gestalten

Contents

Foreword	4
Interviews	
Anagrama	44
Sid Lee	82
Jon Contino	148
Bleed	190
Base Design	226
Kokoro & Moi	266
Address Index	380
Work Index	386
Imprint	400

Foreword

It should be simple. Simple enough to be drawn in the sand with your big toe, as German graphic designer and typographer Kurt Weidemann once claimed. Yet it also has to stand for a large, complex whole. Whether it is for a young start-up or a large multinational corporation, the logo has a paradoxical task. Like the cell of a living creature, it bears within it all the information of the organism. Hence, reduced to the essence of the brand it represents, the logo was long considered untouchable.
With increasing diversification of digital media and ever smaller screens, however, what was long considered impossible now occurs. The once inviolable logo suddenly itself becomes the entity and the point of departure from which other much smaller signs are created.
On the touchpads of smart phones and on browser windows only a few pixels in size, the logo's derivatives now appear as an app button or a favicon. In plain forms, usually with a monochrome palette and with clean lettering, they are merely elements descendant of a proper sign. In short, they are logos of their logo. The smaller signs are intended to provide orientation within the virtual chaos, yet they ensure increasing overstimulation. What does that mean for the logo? Should it adapt to its recent derivatives and become more like the favicon, until it is automatically designed to fit precisely into a 16×16 pixel window? Or, on the contrary, should it become even more complicated and narrative?
Both scenarios currently seem possible and are already underway. Indeed, one potential answer is perplexity: creating confusion seems to be a sure method to stand out on the Internet. In fact, several designers are expressing their enthusiasm toward intellectual logo designs that no longer have much to do with images that can be drawn with your big toe in the sand. Constructed from complex geometric figures and systems, their logos seem subtle and mathematical. Several of them appear in the form of labyrinths, recalling crossword puzzles, sudokus, or cat's cradles. Others, inspired by the impossible spaces of M. C. Escher, Möbius strips, Penrose triangles, and op art paintings, reveal enigmatic dimensional effects and play with optical illusions. Parallel to this trend are those who choose to counter it by

producing clear, straightforward signs. One finds radically reduced monograms, black-and-white contrasts, and striking contours by which these designers try to distinguish themselves from the rest. While new digital tools certainly have their appeal, graphic designers are also looking back on tried-and-true methods. Much like in the arts and crafts movement that emerged in the mid-nineteenth century, there is a romantic yearning for the authentic and original in the current design avant-garde. If it was once a reaction to machine production which was perceived as soulless, today it seems as though it is the cool distance of digital surfaces that is causing this return to traditional craft, archetypical forms, and uniqueness. It is also interesting to notice those who use the newest digital tools to generate the most organic-looking signs: sometimes the more progressive the mediums, the more analog the technique, and the more complex the programs, the more rustic the designs.

The designers countering the dematerialization of objects and the redundant reproduction of content caused by digital progress are doing so by employing engravings and woodcuts, calligraphy, and watercolors. Their subjects are naïve, almost rapturous landscapes, wild plants, and fantastic chimeras. Although one can dive into some of these logos as if into a fairytale, others resemble runes and hieroglyphs, or testify to a more emblematic character. In the shape of coats-of-arms, stamps, or seals, they declare the guilds and traditions of their owners. Here, cutlery, tree trunks, and grains of wheat become symmetrical signets. Anchors or marine creatures decorate restaurant menus, and compositions of needles, scissors, and buttons adorn shirts for contemporary fashion labels. Whether through form or content, they all show that the designer is more than ever a storyteller, as this seventh book in the *Los Logos* series strives to prove. With an international selection of the most recent logo designs—compiled and arranged intuitively—it reveals connections, emphasizes outstanding examples, and gives a foretaste of things to come. Six interviews with leading designers in corporate, logo, and label design offer a look behind the scenes at younger as well as established agencies and at the personalities who enrich our world with inspiring design.

01 Olsson Barbieri

01 Olsson Barbieri

01 Büro Destruct

02 Filmgraphik

03 Live To Make

04 EMPK

01 High Tide

02 Tyler Quarles

03 Feed

04 Floor 5

01 Fuzzco

02 ACRE

03 Intercity

04 Lange & Lange

05 ACRE

06 Cursor Design Studio

10 Typo-Picto

01 Made by Molloy

02 ZEK

03 Studio Moross

04 Gonzalo Rodriguez Gaspar

THE
NORDIC HOUSE
WASHING, DRYING & IRONING

05 Kokoro & Moi

06 Anagrama

01 Chad Michael

02 Brogen Averill

03 Mads Burcharth

04 Dirk Büchsenschütz

01 Codefrisko

02 Frank Aloi

03 Tyrsa

04 Vértice Comunicación

01 Kasper Gram

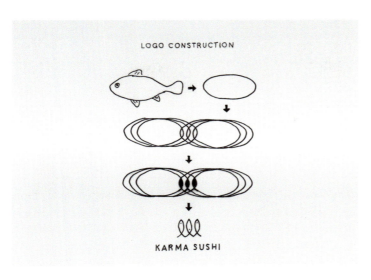

01 Kasper Gram

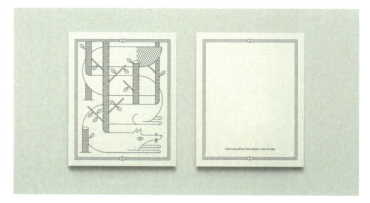

01 Jono Garrett

WILLOW TREE

01 Bunch

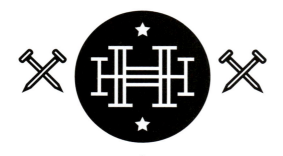

SOUNDKONSTRUKT

02 903 Creative

03 Aro

01 brandmor

02 Hovercraft Studio

03 Bureau Lukas Haider

01 Sid Lee

BALDWIN HARRIS

01 Magpie Studio

02 Berger & Föhr

03 Booth

BLUE GOOSE

01 Sid Lee

THE ONLY ADDITIVE WE USE IS LOVE.

01 Pedro Paulino

02 Kokoro & Moi

03 QOOP

04 Alter

24 Typo

- ESTAB/13 -
FOOD OF THE PEOPLE
BADUZZI
finest hand-made meatballs
ITALIAN INSPIRED FOOD & WINE
- Corner Jellicoe Street & Fish Lane -
NORTH WHARF AUCKLAND

01 One Design

PEE
ACE

01 Albert Naasner

FINS
INSTITUT
CULTUREEL
CULTUREL
INSTITUUT
FINLANDAIS

02 Kokoro & Moi

BERLIN
PARIS

03 BUREAU Mario Lombardo

04 ACRE

BARTU & SPITZENBERGER

01 Bureau Mirko Borsche

02 DAS.Graphiker

TOMWOOD

03 Anagrama

04 Bleed

01 Till Paukstat

02 Torrents

03 Re-public

04 Daniele Politini

05 Andrew Woodhead

01 laboratoř

02 Swear Words

03 Dimomedia Lab

04 Walter Giordano

05 Trademark?

06 A-Side Studio

tatianqueiroz

01 Aristu & Co

DOMĒSTICO

02 Manifiesto Futura

03 Konstantinos Gargaletsos

DESERTMED

04 Eps51 Graphic Design Studio

COURTESY

05 Akatre

DEVAMBEZ
GRAVEUR · ÉDITEUR D'ART

06 ZeCraft

BOLÍVAR

07 Heydays

DEAR ROUGE

01 Fivethousand Fingers

1981

02 Albert Naasner

schlecht™

PLUSH

04 &Larry

LA SKÉNÉT'EAU

03 Wanja Ledowski

EAT—HOLA

05 Konstantinos Gargaletsos

NOSIVE STRUKTURE

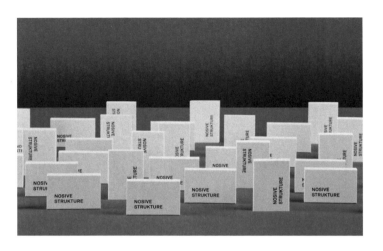

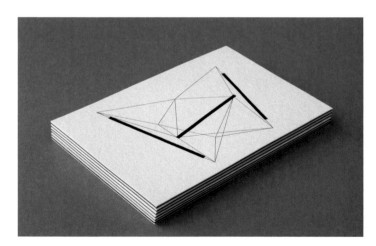

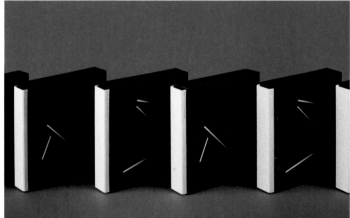

01 Bunch

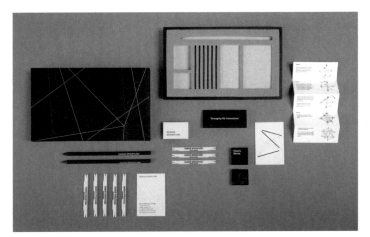
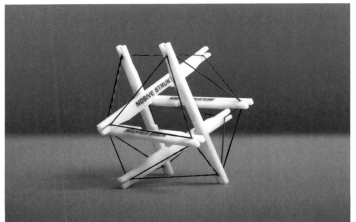

01 Bunch

TWL™

01 Jaemin Lee

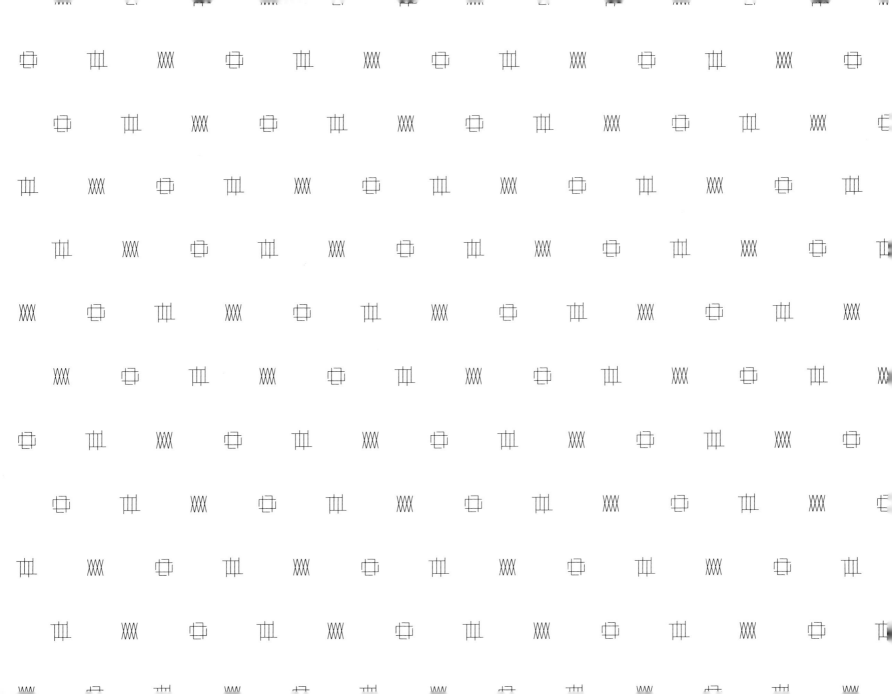

01 Passport

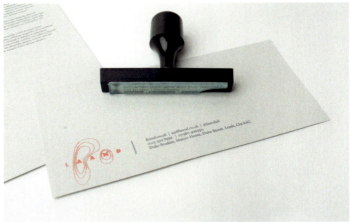

01 Passport

01 CHRISTIANCONLH

02 Core60

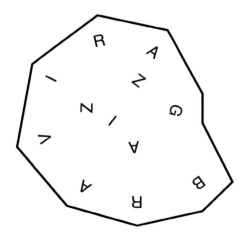

03 Edgar Bąk

Terra Mare Conservation

01 Fuzzco

02 Erik Kiesewetter

01 Coup

01 Di-Da

02 Fontan 2

03 Fuzzco

04 Anti

01 HappyMess Studio

02 Gianmarco Magnani

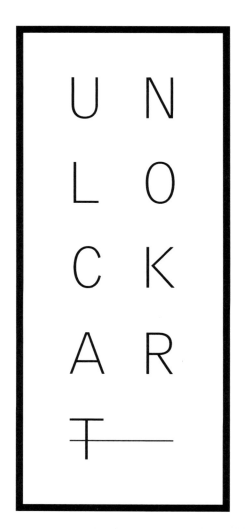

03 Konstantinos Gargaletsos

01 Hüfner Design

02 Fivethousand Fingers

03 Codefrisko

04 Bureau Lukas Haider

05 C1AU.AS.KEE

Anagrama

Sebastian Padilla (creative director)
Lucía Elizondo (production designer)

Interweaving multidisciplinary design services with business expertise, Anagrama extends beyond the traditional concept of a creative agency. Since 2008, the young Mexico-based team has been taking on projects ranging from branding to software and multimedia design. Clients from all over the world and in varied industries call on Anagrama, as they are well versed in fields as different as those of architecture, fashion, and food. Sebastian Padilla is the co-founder and creative director of the studio, while Lucía Elizondo is responsible for production design.

What does Anagrama do?
We create a balance between a design boutique that focuses on the development of creative pieces with the utmost attention to detail and a business consultancy firm that provides solutions based on the analysis of tangible data.

You are still under 30. What drove you to create your own company?
We decided to start a studio in order to have more creative independence, earn more money, and be able to have bigger and better projects that are important on an international level.

How does your studio's name represent your work methods?
The word "anagram" means arranging things in different ways to produce a new meaning. We always strive to create something unique by drawing inspiration from the most unlikely sources. The name also has a really nice ring to it.

How would you describe the Anagrama style?
It's clean in a visual sense: all the elements in our projects have a reason for being where they are, as the visual composition is always based on the brand's needs and a solid concept.

What makes a brand beautiful?
Close attention to detail.

Which analog and digital techniques do you use?
We always start with hand-drawn sketches. It allows us to be more flexible and helps us generate more ideas faster. Then we turn to whatever software is appropriate for each project.

How do you apply color to underline the meaning of a brand?
We use color as a primary tool to organize, systemize, or simply add highlights to something that is very sober and clean. We love that formula. It's kind of our trademark.

You often use elaborate draperies and poetic imagery for the corporate designs you create. What about the other senses, aside from the visual?
We know that the more recognizable aspects a brand has, the stronger it becomes. This doesn't only apply on a visual level, it includes elements such as sounds and smells as well. So we try to incorporate these extra elements as much as possible. Working on a project, especially a multidisciplinary one that includes interior design for example, we aim for an experience that transcends visuals. For instance, Theurel & Thomas, the French macaroon patisserie, must always smell a little like sweet almond paste, not like a citrus plug-in scent or some other clashing scent, and the music must be tranquil and at a soft volume. Montero, on the other hand, a restaurant in the desert, should have a more rugged ambiance such as a rosemary scent and slightly louder music.

What does the interior design of your studio look like?
It's a revamped warehouse space. The floor is polished concrete. Some walls are whitewashed blocks, the others black drywall, and the air conditioning vents on the black ceiling are neon yellow, which creates a really cool effect, almost as if the vents were floating.

What does daily life in your studio look like?
We have two offices, one in Monterrey and one in Mexico City. There are about thirty people working at the Monterrey offices and five in Mexico City. The ages range from 23 to 33 years old, so we're mostly young people. We're not just co-workers, we have a great time together and not just at the office. We often go out to eat or drink just like any group of friends.

Do you have an idol?
We have several, like Josef Müller-Brockmann and Mies van der Rohe, off the top of my head. We appreciate attention to detail and the Swiss-like devotion to order and cleanliness.

Which job are you most proud of?
Theurel & Thomas was the project that launched us into the international design community. It gave us credibility and made us competitive on an international level.
Sofía was a great project as well. It set new standards for us. It was a huge project with a fantastic client who had a good budget and complete trust in us. I think that would be any designer's dream: to have the freedom to create without any limitations.

Which client would you like to work for next?
We'd love to work for an airline or a big hotel.

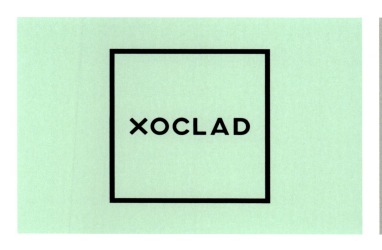

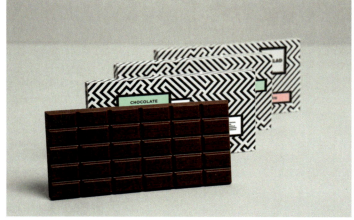

01 Anagrama

01 Anagrama

01 Clase Bcn

02 hopa studio

CONTENT & CONTAINER

03 Kokoro & Moi

04 Bureau Bleen

01 Studio No. 10

02 HappyMess Studio

03 Bureau Lukas Haider

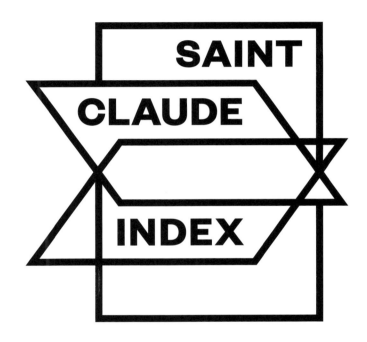

04 Erik Kiesewetter

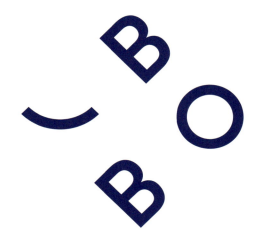

European
Holiday Home
Association

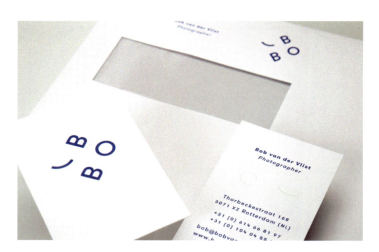

01 Kursiv

02 Pony Design Club

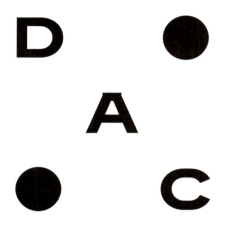

01 Kokoro & Moi

02 Onlab

03 Neeser & Müller

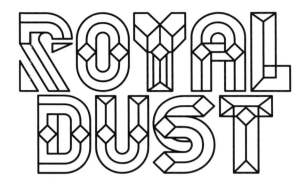

01 MASA

02 Matt W. Moore

COLOGNE SESSIONS

03 Hugo Hoppmann

01 Vallée Duhamel

02 Matt Le Gallez

joa
qui
m

po
r
tela

ar
quite
tos

03 R2 Design

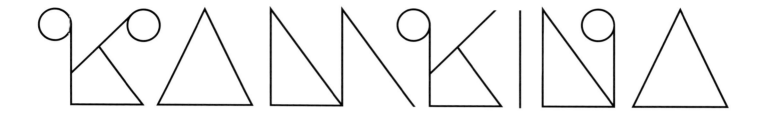

PARIS — ST. PETERSBURG

01 Mr Walczuk

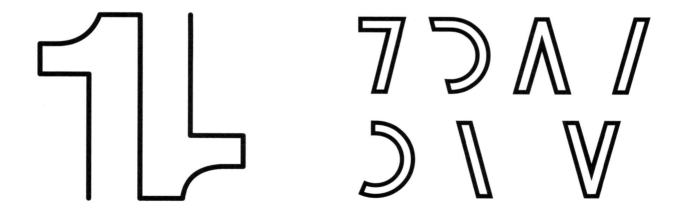

02 Signers

03 Anti

01 Mr. Magenta

02 Chris Rubino

03 Longton

01 Büro Glöwing

02 Tobias Munk

03 David Büsser

04 Olivier Charland

05 Jochen Kuckuck

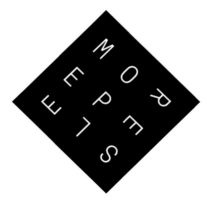

06 MoreSleep

01 The Simple Society

02 Martin Silvestre

03 Verena Michelitsch

04 QOOP

05 DADADA studio

06 Anagrama

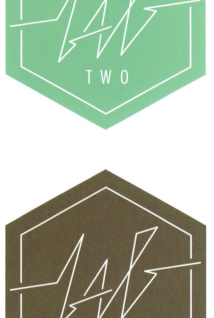

01 Lab-2

01 Inkgraphix

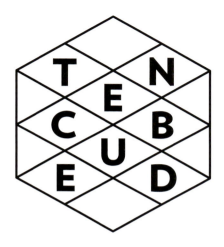

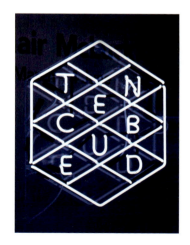

01 Alter

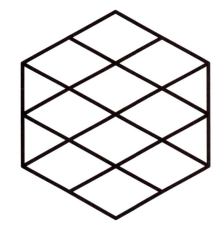
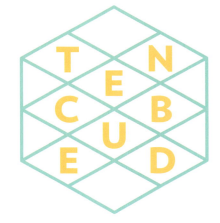

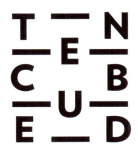
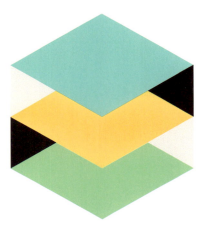

01 Alter

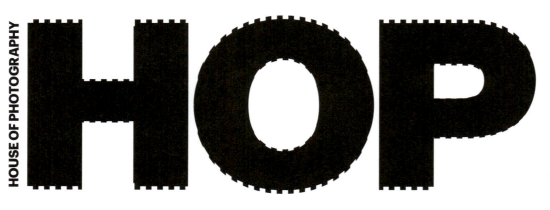

01 &Larry

62 Typo-Playful

01 GOOQX

02 Name and Name

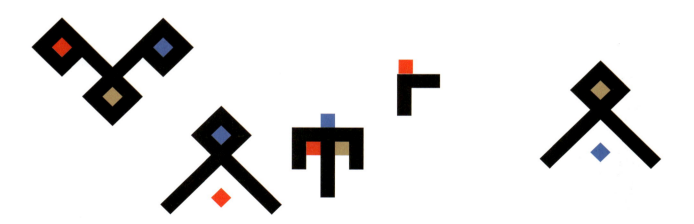

03 Acme Industries

01 Dainippon Type Organization

01 Fontan 2

02 HappyMess Studio

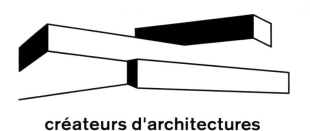

01 Andrea Münch

02 George Popov

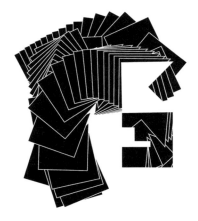

03 Gianni Rossi

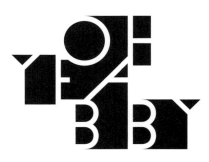

04 Pedro Paulino

01 Open Studio

 Semperoper Dresden

 Semperoper Junge Szene

 Semperoper Ballett

01 Fons Hickmann m23

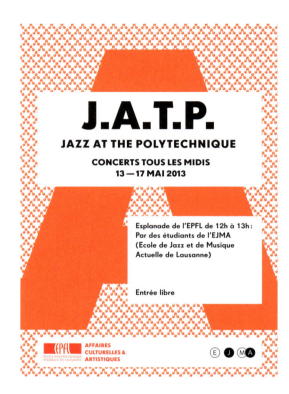

01 Fulguro

01 Fulguro

01 Fontan 2

02 e-Types A/S

03 Deutsche & Japaner

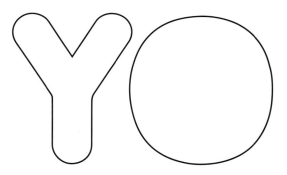

04 Mr. Magenta

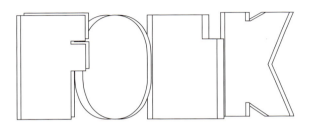

01 Mr. Magenta

02 AIM Studio

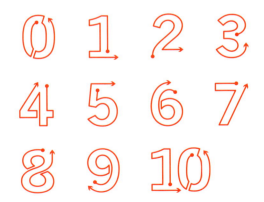

03 Post Typography

01 Kissmiklos

02 fjopus7

03 Coup

04 C1AU.AS.KEE

01 Raum Mannheim

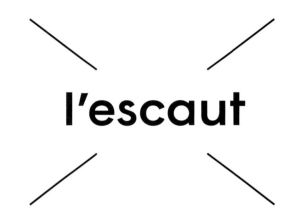

02 Salutpublic

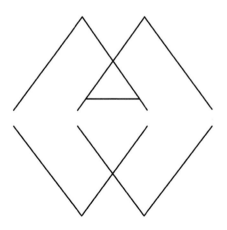

03 Richard Baird

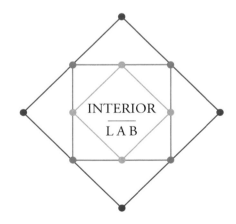

04 Graphinya

01 Mr Walczuk

02 Core60

03 Two Times Elliott

04 Face

01 Live To Make

02 Tim Boelaars

03 Milosz Klimek

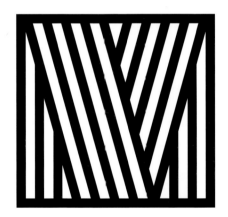

04 José Design

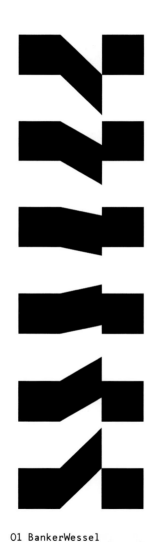

02 IS Creative Studio

01 BankerWessel

03 Two Times Elliott

01 Hype Type Studio

02 Tomato

03 José Design

04 Rob Angermuller

05 Fabio Milito Design

06 Two Times Elliott

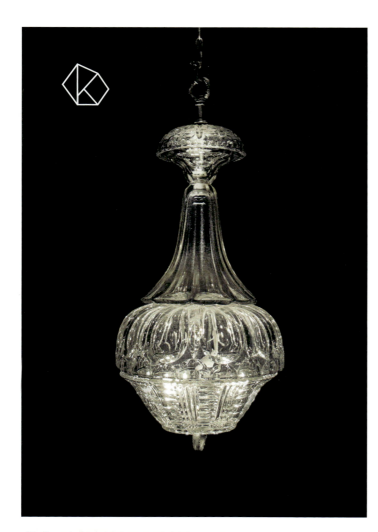

01 Jonas Ganz

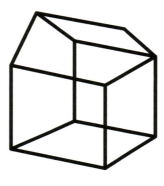

AP.ART

02 Francis Elias

kando

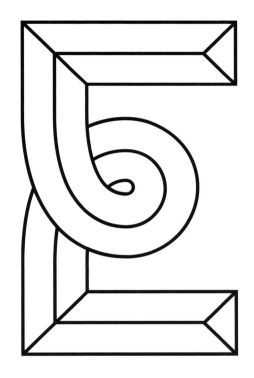

02 Pedro Paulino

ENGRAIN

01 Swear Words

Sid Lee

Philippe Meunier (chief creative officer)

With almost 600 employees in offices in Montréal, Amsterdam, Paris, Toronto, and New York, along with a global client base, Sid Lee is a leading creative agency when it comes to strategic communication concepts and costumer experiences. Founded in 1993, services range from branding to architecture. Philippe Meunier, co-founder and chief creative officer, was responsible for the new ADC (Art Directors Club) identity.

Congratulations! For the fourth time Sid Lee was voted Agency of the Year. Why?
We are trying to make things different. Winning Agency of the Year isn't only about doing great work but also about trying to transform the industry, which I think we are starting to get recognized for.

Last year Sid Lee had its 20th anniversary. How did you celebrate?
We didn't really throw a party... We did a 20th version of our ridiculous yearly moron awards to celebrate 20 years of craziness.

As chief creative officer of Sid Lee you compare yourself to a farmer. What can you tell us about biodiversity?
I like to compare our creative directors to farmers since they have to walk around the field every morning to make sure we are growing the best and freshest product. We like to grow different types in the same field, because it's by planting tomatoes next to basil that you will affect the taste and make things interesting. It is important for them to contaminate one another in order to create something unique.

What are "creative flavors"?
The more you travel and the more you see and taste, the more creative an agency will be.

What is the difference between a farm, a studio, and an atelier?
A studio is where people create and produce, and an atelier is where you create and craft. This is why we call our Sid Lee offices ateliers.

Why is it so important to be a "crafter" at Sid Lee?
Because I believe that our work is loaded with emotion.

What is a good idea?
A good idea is something you can understand from a small Post-it and that can be stuck on anything.

You developed a signet resembling Albrecht Dürer's monogram for the New York-based Art Directors Club. Dürer always fought against plagiarism. How do you defend your copy?
The reason ADC has used Albrecht Dürer's signature as the inspiration for their logo for 93 years is because they wanted to honor him and pay him tribute. Albrecht is credited for being the first commercial artist in the world and his work is the epitome of craft. To commercialize and distribute art is also ADC's mission. Our version is an evolution of the first logo.

Sid Lee is in corporate design, social marketing, advertising, products, spaces, and retail design. What will come next?
Live entertainment, because I believe that brands are now ready to move out of the screen and out of mobile applications. Anything that is about theatre, dance, and street art performance really catches my attention.

How do you create "stuff people love to talk about"*?
If you create stuff that will transform a consumer experience, people will love to share. Human beings like to show off their intelligence, therefore give them the opportunity to do so.

Do we need another story?
Yes. We constantly need to reinvent our industry because creativity is an exciting field and there is no end to it.

*See: Cesvet, Bertrand, Tony Babinski, and Eric Alper. Conversational Capital: How to Create Stuff People Love to Talk about. Upper Saddle River, NJ: FT Press, 2009.

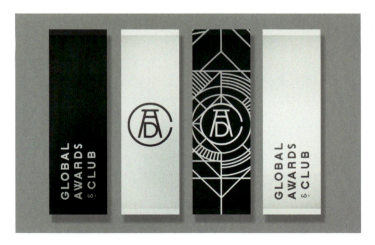

01 Sid Lee

01 Sid Lee

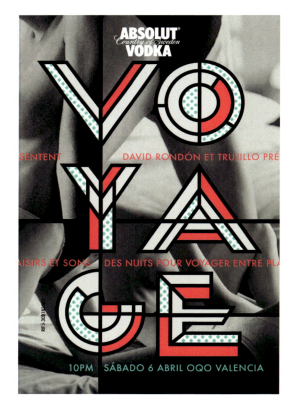

01 Emil Hartvig

02 Nohemi Dicuru

SERRE NUMÉRIQUE

01 Atelier télescopique

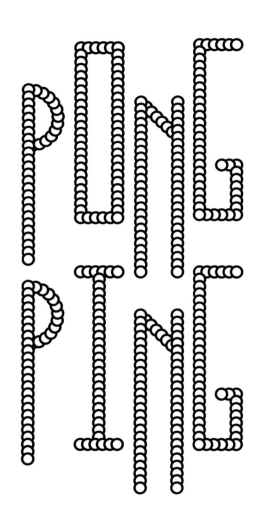

01 Dave Sedgwick

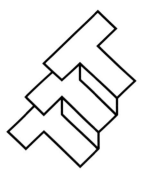

**Twenty
TwentyTwo**

01 Dave Sedgwick

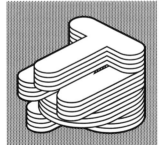

02 TNOP

03 Paul Coors

04 Dave Sedgwick

Typo-Playful 89

ECHTWALD

ECHTWALD

ECHTWALD

ECHTWALD

ECHTWALD

ECHTWALD

ECHTWALD

ECHTWALD

01 Double Standards

01 ACRE

02 Intercity

Family 91

01 Kommerz

 FYSIEKE INTEGRITEIT

 ACTIEF BURGERSCHAP

 DUURZAAM VAKMANSCHAP

 BREDE VAKANTIESCHOOL

01 Kommerz

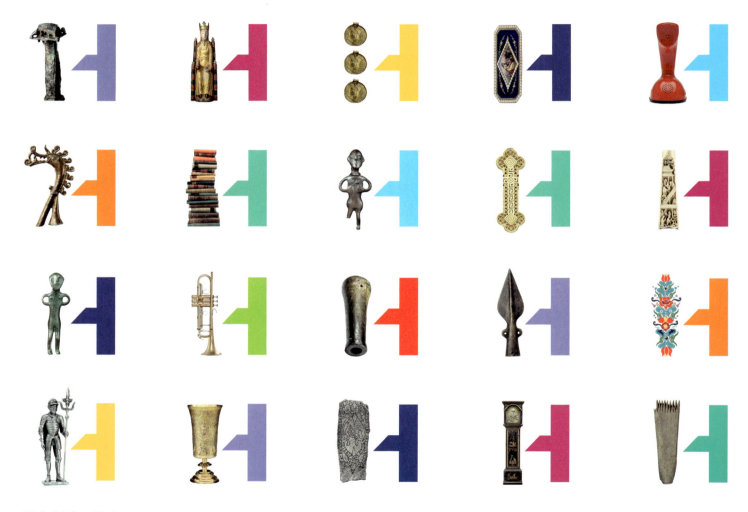

01 Bold Stockholm

94 Family

01 Salutpublic

CLARIANT

  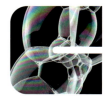 

01 Mutabor Design

01 Mutabor Design

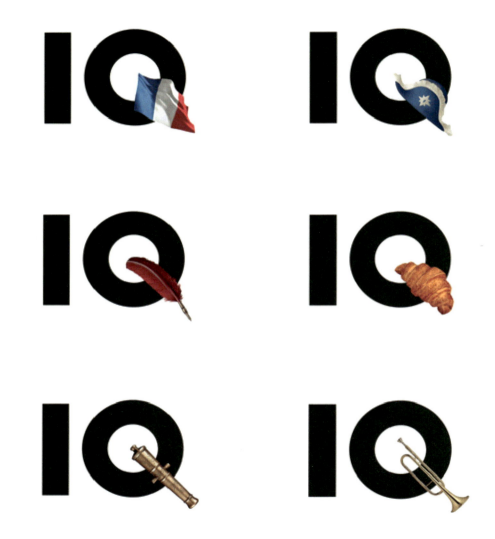

01 Smart Heart

01 Johan Thuresson

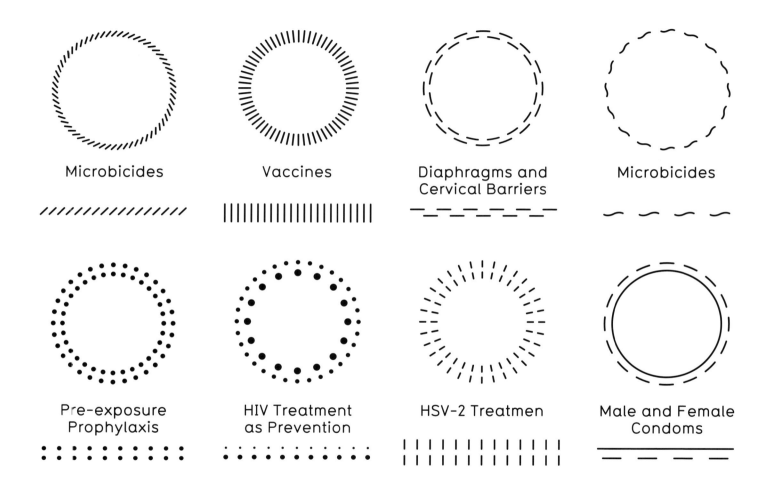

01 COOEE Graphic Design

100 Family

01 Quinta-Feira

01 Fulguro

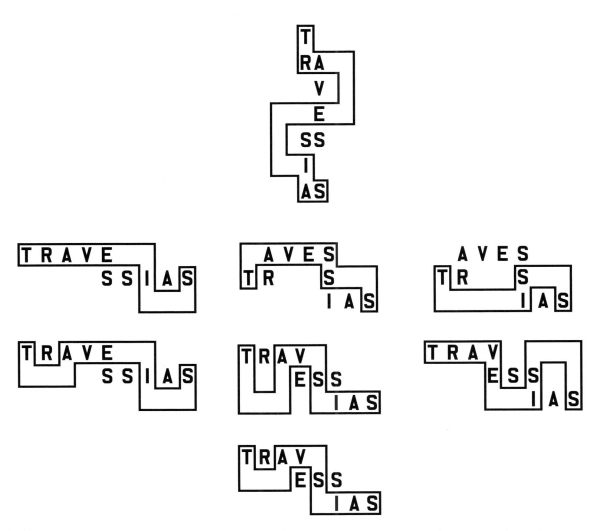

01 Quinta-Feira

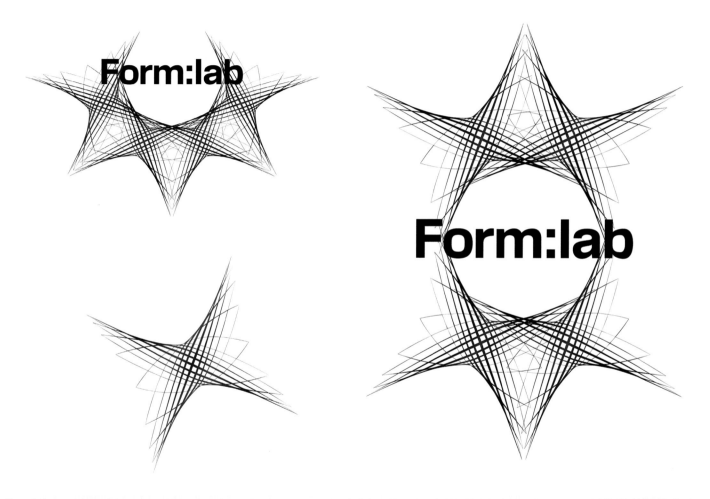

01 Kursiv

01 Mutabor Design

01 Jacknife

01 Jacknife

Animals 107

01 Bunch

02 Steven Bonner

03 Codefrisko

04 Christian Rothenhagen

108 Animals

01 HappyMess Studio

02 Surface

03 Rickey Lindberg

04 Roy Smith

01 Floor 5

02 Bergfest

03 Alen 'Type08' Pavlovic

04 Full Color Canvas

110 Animals

01 Jochen Kuckuck

02 10 Associates

03 ZEK

04 Noeeko

01 Roman Kirichenko

02 Stitch Design Co.

03 Josiah Jost

04 image now

112 Animals

01 GrandArmy

02 DADADA studio

03 Trademark?

04 Christian Rothenhagen

01 Down With Design

02 André Beato

03 backyard 10

114 Animals

01 Fuzzco

02 Signers

03 Hype Type Studio

04 Tropenelektronik

01 Das Buro

02 Roy Smith

01 BRANDED

01 Partly Sunny

02 Salon91

03 indyvisuals

04 Maximilian Baud

118 Animals

01 Chad Michael

02 indyvisuals

03 Julian Hrankov

04 The National Grid

01 Thonik

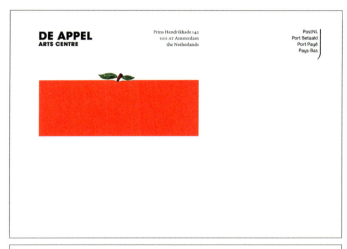

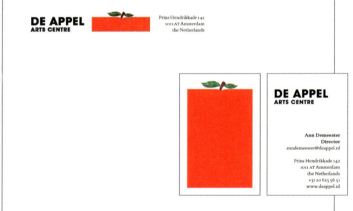

01 Thonik

01 Swear Words

02 Mondbewohner

03 Face

04 Non-Format

122 Abstract

OCEAN MADE SEAFOOD

01 Swear Words

02 Noeeko

THE NEW NEW

03 Andrea Münch

04 Cerotreees

05 Bleed

01 Gravit Art

HELSINKI FOOD COMPANY

02 Werklig

03 Fontan 2

04 Tabas

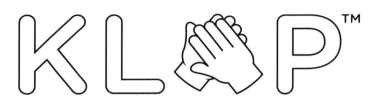

KLEINTIERPRAXIS
M. RUSCH

01 Rickey Lindberg

02 David Büsser

BERGISCHE WAREN

HAUS
Inc.

03 zumquadrat

04 UNIT

01 David Büsser

02 Eps51 Graphic Design Studio

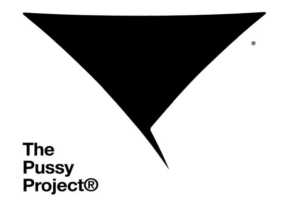

01 Mr Walczuk

02 Fons Hickmann m23

03 Tomato Kosir

01 Aro

02 Sasha Prood

03 Conspiracy Studio

04 La Tortillería

01 Sunday Vision

02 NNNNY

03 Mash

04 Büro Destruct

CATCH INSPIRED
PORTLAND, ORE

01 Hovercraft Studio

01 The National Grid

02 THINKMULE

03 Kanardo

04 Kanardo

01 fjopus7

02 Olivier Charland

THE
GOOD FISH CO.

03 Swear Words

04 R2 Design

01 Patrick Molnar

01 The National Grid

02 THINKMULE

03 Pierpaolo Scarpato

04 Inventaire

01 Ryan Feerer

02 ACRE

03 Dennis Herzog

04 De Jongens Ronner

01 Funnel: Eric Kass

02 Ryan Feerer

03 Chad Michael

04 Vértice Comunicación

01 RUBÉN B

02 Jono Garrett

03 Jochen Kuckuck

04 Chad Michael

01 Akinori Oishi

02 44flavours

03 Hula + Hula Design

01 Work-N-Roll

02 Maniackers Design

03 44flavours

04 Studio Moross

05 Cindy T. Mai

01 Eduardo Vidales

02 MASA

Cream Colored Ponies

Nr. 000

01 Hort

01 Struggle inc.

02 SELLOUT INDUSTRIES

03 Jochen Kuckuck

01 Nicholaus Jamieson

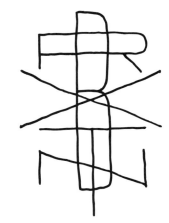

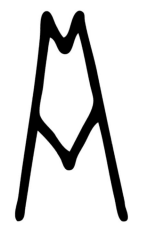

02 Albert Naasner

03 Struggle inc.

01 44flavours

02 Akinori Oishi

03 George Popov

01 Chragokyberneticks

02 Di-Da

03 44flavours

02 Noeeko-Design Studio

01 Noeeko

03 HappyMess Studio

01 Bergfest

02 IS Creative Studio

03 Trademark?

Jon Contino

Jon Contino

Jon Contino virtuously combines traditional styles and handmade letterings with street art elements and digital techniques. That is how the young New York City-based designer creates nostalgic worlds and gives contemporary labels a charming historic aura.

Could you please tell us who Jon Contino is?
I'm a designer, illustrator, lettering artist, creative director... the list goes on and on. I grew up in New York and still live and work here to this day. I work in advertising, branding, and men's fashion.

You call yourself an "Alphastructaesthetitologist." What does this mean?
It's kind of an obnoxious response that I give when people ask what I do. These days it's hard to really describe what designers do because we have to do so many different things. Broken down, "Alphastructaesthetitologist" means "one who studies and designs by using the art of letterforms." It also kind of means nothing at the same time.

What would you be if you had not become an artist?
It would be a long shot, but I would love to be a professional baseball player. I've always had an obsession for baseball and that would be my first choice.

You have a lot of tattoos. What is the difference between skin, paper, and a screen?
There's not really much difference. The idea of collecting tattoos to tell a story is something that really appeals to me. Whether you intend to or not, piecing them together tells a certain personal history, and to me, the concept of visual storytelling is the most amazing thing human beings are capable of. Even though the canvas changes, it doesn't change the purpose.

What do you read? Which films do you like? What kind of art inspires you?
I'm not much of a reader, I just don't have the patience. Movies in general are something I love because it has that same kind of visual storytelling that I'm so obsessed with. Specifically though I love *Ghostbusters* and *The Godfather*. Those two are my all-time favorites. I also love cheesy eighties horror movies and comedies. In terms of art, it all inspires me. You can see what it's like to exist through another person's eyes.

What does your work space look like?
There are walls covered in artworks, bookshelves filled with my obsessions, samples of products all over, and a small shrine to the New York Yankees lining half the studio.

What does craftsmanship mean to you?
Having a desire to make something and making it, regardless of the limitations in front of you.

What are the techniques you use for your illustrations?
I try to be as organic as possible. Let my hand do the talking for me. If there's a mistake, I leave it in. It's really important to me to be able to feel the emotion in my work and anything that takes away from that has to be eliminated.

Does a good designer necessarily have to be able to draw?
Not necessarily. I know a few really great designers that can't draw at all, but I think they're freaks of nature. It's pretty vital to be able to draw and get your ideas on paper in some way, but I have to say the guys I know that can't draw also understand composition exceptionally well. That's what makes it work for them.

Why do you think so many brands count on retro styles and nostalgic motifs at the moment?
A handful of great brands are handling either nostalgia or legitimate history in a very delicate, precise way. But many others don't put forth the effort to understand the history behind either the design or their own brand and think that a vintage design will automatically give them credibility. It's not the case. They only jump on the bandwagon turning it into a watered down movement of mediocrity.

German graphic designer and typographer Kurt Weidemann once said that a logo is good if you can draw it in the sand with your big toe. Your labels are comparatively complex. How would you respond to this?
It's important to note that label design and logo design are two very different things. You can definitely get away with more complex designs in labels because they need to contain much more information. My logo work is remarkably more pared down than my label work, and that's simply because it can say more with less. It's funny though, because I feel that all of my work (logos included) is still relatively simple. There may be many elements involved, but most of it is simply black marks on white paper.

Creation often means citing former artists. Are you copying?
Absolutely not. I have hundreds of influences that I've packed into my brain and they definitely play a part into how I design, but my choices are based on how I feel about the context of each project. My work is always a combination of these ideas thrown together. The basis of human creative culture is to learn from those who came before you and build on top of what they made. That's how we all get better at what we do.

01 Jon Contino

01 Jon Contino

01 Tyrsa

02 Toshikazu Nozaka

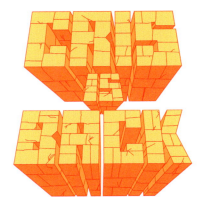

01 Cless

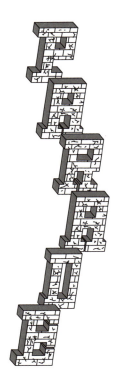

02 designJune

03 Sammy Stein

01 SELLOUT INDUSTRIES

02 Dr. Morbito

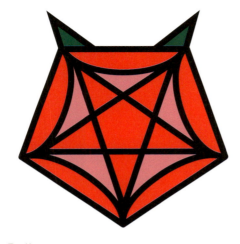

01 Cindy T. Mai

02 Modo

01 Finsta

02 Cutts Creative

03 Braca Burazeri

04 Laundry

05 designJune

01 FÖRM

02 Alfredo Conrique

03 Aldo Lugo

04 Jacques et Brigitte

05 THINKMULE

01 Albert Naasner

02 Hula + Hula Design

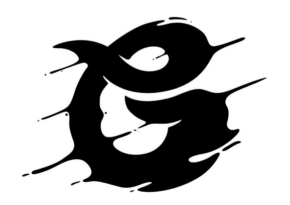

03 Gonzalo Rodriguez Gaspar

04 Vier5

01 Anna Magnussen

02 ['ændi:] Andrea Romano

03 Shinpei Onishi

AQUILES

01 cabina 02 Csaba Bernáth

03 Anarchy Alchemy 04 Paul Coors

DENHAM

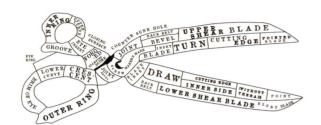

DENHAM

01 Denham

WHO THE FUCK IS EL SOLITARIO?

01 El Solitario

01 El Solitario

01 Chragokyberneticks

02 alessandridesign

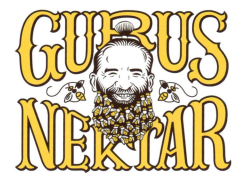

01 Typejockeys

02 designJune

03 Andreas Klammt

04 Teacake Design

01 alessandridesign

02 Noeeko

03 THINKMULE

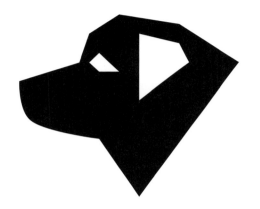

01 Berger & Föhr

02 OMOCHI

03 Max-o-matic

04 Jonathan Calugi

01 Live To Make

02 Tim Boelaars

03 Tim Bjørn

04 Triboro Design

01 Jonathan Calugi

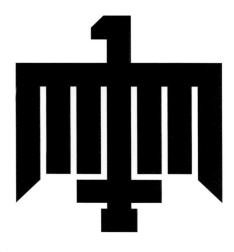

01 Face

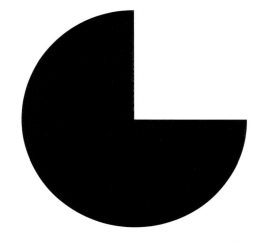

02 Vonsung

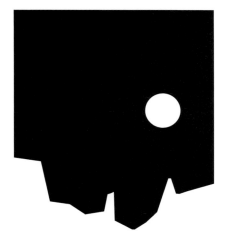

03 Friedrich Santana Lamego

04 Tridente Brand Firm

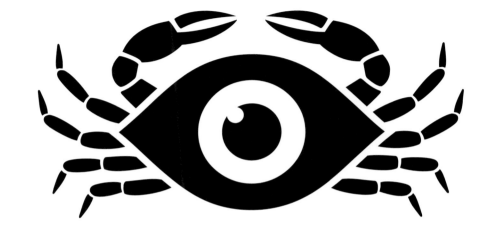

01 Tobias Munk

02 Mehdi Saeedi   03 Sawdust   04 Rob Angermuller   05 Tim Boelaars

01 Milosz Klimek

01 Milosz Klimek   02 Live To Make

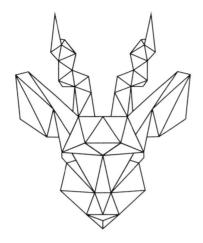

01 310k

02 Stefano Bracci

03 mañana communication

04 Atelier Dessert

01 Heroes Design

02 brandmor

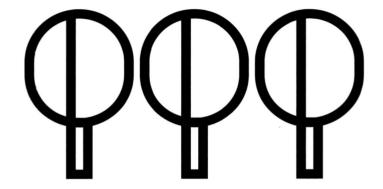
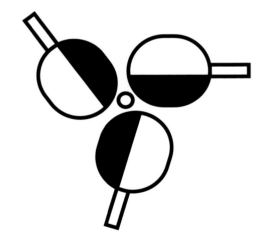

01 Zweizehn

02 100und1

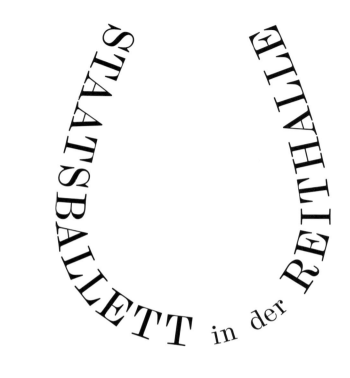

STAATSBALLETT in der REITHALLE

MUSE-UM
OFF
MUSE-UM

01 Bureau Mirko Borsche

02 BUREAU Mario Lombardo

ROOM
SERVICE

ROMEO
GIULIA

03 Heroes Design

04 minigram

this monster

01 Julianna Goodman

RUST

02 RUBÉN B

03 Canefantasma Studio   04 Kissmiklos

01 Kissmiklos

02 Laundry

03 Andreas Neophytou

04 Deanne Cheuk

05 Kissmiklos

01 Kissmiklos

cielo SPA

———————————————

01 cabina

Sounds
of
Silence

02 Desres Design Group

03 Kissmiklos

comm/unique

7/SUITES

01 Vonsung

02 minigram

NEUER
SCHÜTZENHOF

SPIRIT

03 minigram

04 cabina

FOOD & ———

01 Passport

twentytwenty

01 Sociodesign

02 Family

03 Homework

EXTRAVIRGEN

01 Manifiesto Futura

KUĆA

02 Longton

VENKAVISION
for every season

03 Kissmiklos

EDWARDA

04 Wanja Ledowski

ever rêve

05 Lundgren+Lindqvist

zerzer.
ceramics

06 Maximilian Baud

vom guten wohnen.

07 unfolded

01 Manifiesto Futura

02 Fivethousand Fingers

03 Anagrama

04 Anti/Anti

05 Bureau Mirko Borsche

06 Homework

07 ANONIMO STUDIO

08 Josiah Jost

01 Tom Grant

02 brandmor

03 Zeroipocrisia

04 ZeCraft

05 Homework

06 Werklig

07 Deutsche & Japaner

08 Côme de Bouchony

186 Typo-Serif

The Independent Magazine

01 ZeCraft

02 Filmgraphik

THE GERMANS

03 Bureau Mirko Borsche

Macaulay Sinclair

04 Studio Output

Billie Sunday

05 Antonio Ladrillo

06 Swear Words

custommade

01 Honework

costaoeste

02 Face

fripan®

03 Espluga+Associates

manuscritics

04 erretres.

http:))

05 Pedro Paulino

sleek

06 BUREAU Mario Lombardo

panthalassa

07 Salon91

frida

08 Espluga+Associates

01 Kissmiklos

02 Alex Trochut

BLCKMRKT

03 SANSCOLOR

Le Monde

04 ZeCraft

mesnetsiz

05 Gravit Art

Buynachten

06 genauso.und.anders

Bleed

Svein Haakon Lia (creative director / founding partner)

Founded in 2000 by Svein Haakon Lia and Dag Solhaug Laska, Bleed is a multidisciplinary design consultancy with visual identity as its core business. Their offices in Oslo and Vienna serve clients such as Ikea, Myspace, and Pepsi. In this interview, Lia explains what his design work has to do with his navel, a floating plastic swan, and apples.

Bleed, where does the name come from?
Bleed began as a whimsical revolution within graphic design and the name was meant to have two meanings: "bleed for the revolution" but also the edge that you would normally cut away, the bleed.

What did you do before you created your company?
There were five of us who started Bleed back in 2000. All of us came from good positions in quite large design and technology companies. We all wanted new challenges but were unable to find a place where we really wanted to work. So we decided to create our own company with our own ideals and manifesto.

Why haven't you become an artist?
I lack the patience and discipline to look at my own navel too long.

What role do new technologies play in your work?
Technology makes the world smaller and gives us the freedom to try out our ideas and visions with ease.

What do you see when you look out of your studio window?
We are fortunate to be in the center of Oslo but still have nature right outside the window. So we see trees, a river, and a bridge. Very calming. It is also worth mentioning that there is an artwork of a plastic swan shaped as a penis floating in the river and a classic golden angel statue on the other side. Can't ask for more.

What sits on your desk?
It is messy at times, but you'll always find my headset, my sketchbook, and a bottle of water.

What does success mean to you?
It is the calm after a well-executed project.

What does failure mean to you?
"Failure is the condiment that gives success its flavor."
– Truman Capote

Who is in the detail: God or the devil?
Neither. The details are in the details.

On your website you quote the dramatist George Bernard Shaw: "If you have an apple and I have an apple and we exchange these apples then you and I will still each have one apple. But if you have an idea and I have an idea and we exchange these ideas, then each of us will have two ideas." What roles do cooperation and sharing play for you?
There is little point in producing design in a vacuum. We need to see, experience, and share what we do. Bleed's culture is based upon the process of working together toward the same end. That is how we achieve the small and large revolutions for our clients and for ourselves.

ANDREAS KLEIBERG

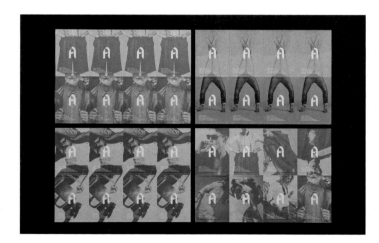

01 SANSCOLOR

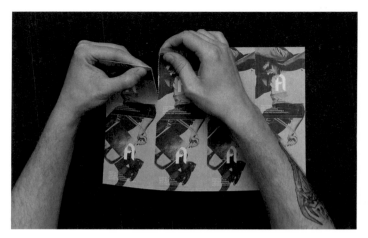

01 SANSCOLOR

01 Por Amor al Arte

02 Onlab

03 zumquadrat

04 Ross Gunter

05 Kissmiklos

01 cabina

02 Aro

03 Codefrisko

04 Pony Design Club

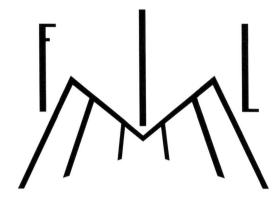

01 BUREAU Mario Lombardo

02 Tom Hingston Studio

03 Denis März

04 ['ændi:] Andrea Romano

01 Rüdiger Götz

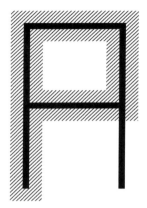

02 R2 Design

03 Full Color Canvas

04 Wanja Ledowski

01 Tyrsa

02 André Beato

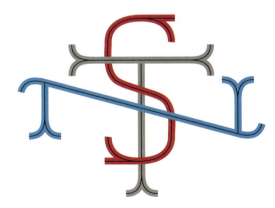

03 Denis März

04 Anagrama

05 Dennis Herzog

01 Bureau Lukas Haider

02 Magpie Studio

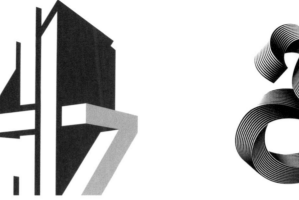

03 Alex Trochut

04 Jon Contino

05 indyvisuals

01 Alex Trochut

02 Tyrsa

03 Tyrsa

04 Kissmiklos

01 Andrei Robu

02 Moker

03 Brendan Prince

01 Fons Hickmann m23

02 Glenn Garriock

03 Identity

01 Linnea Blixt

02 The National Grid

03 Chad Michael

04 Stier Royal

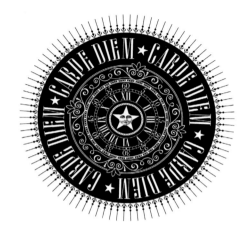

01 Anna-OM-line

02 Teacake Design

03 Acme Industries

04 Live To Make

01 Stitch Design Co.

02 Funnel: Eric Kass

03 Mr. Brown

04 Cutts Creative

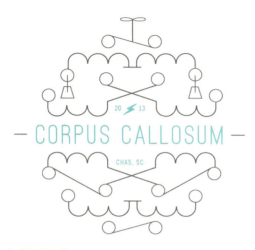

01 Stitch Design Co.

02 Csaba Bernáth

03 Maniackers Design

04 Josiah Jost

02 La Tortillería

01 alessandridesign

03 Olsson Barbieri

01 Hovard Design

02 Conspiracy Studio

03 Aro

04 Kissmiklos

01 GOOQX

02 Bo Lundberg

03 Base

04 Estudio Soma

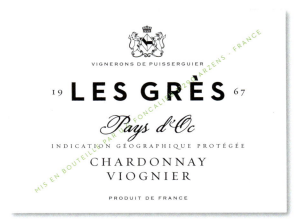

01 Olsson Barbieri

01 Chad Michael

02 Hovard Design

03 Fuzzco

04 MM75 Design

Buddha's Tea

01 PolkaGrafik

BOUQUETTA
ФЛОРИСТИЧНИЙ САЛОН

02 Graphinya

03 Escobas

04 Studio AH-HA

01 Rickey Lindberg

02 Yotam Bezalel Studio

03 Daniel Blik

04 Lange & Lange

01 Stitch Design Co.

02 De Jongens Ronner

03 Roxane Lagache

01 Irving & Co

02 Matt Vergotis

03 Teacake Design

04 DADADA studio

01 Roberto Funke

02 Aro

03 Verena Michelitsch

04 Studio AH-HA

05 Drach P. Claude

01 Studio AH-HA

02 Tomato

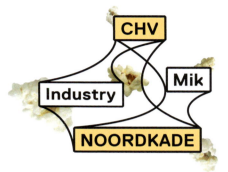 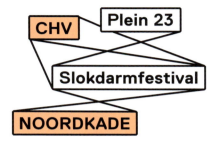 

01 Edhv

02 Christine Vallaure

218 Typo-Framed

01 ZEK

L-ARCHITECTES

01 Fulguro

02 Tomato Kosir

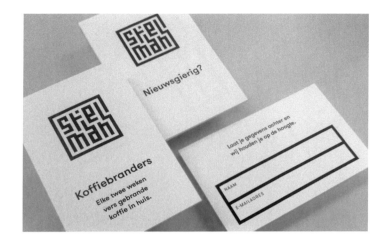

01 Pony Design Club

02 Hort

01 Côme de Bouchony

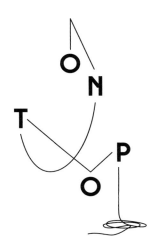

02 HappyMess Studio

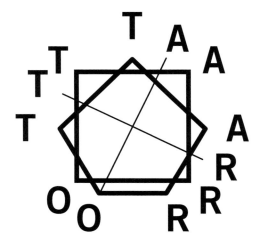

03 LLdesign

```
B           B                    EDITION B
A           A                            A
U           U                            U
H           H                            H
A           A                            A
U           U                            U
S           S KOLLEG                     S
A
U
S

D
E
S
S
A
U
```

01 Hort

01 Lundgren+Lindqvist — THE ARCHIVE PHOTOGRAPHIC

02 Núria Vila — L'ENCANT

03 Thonik — SONSBEEK / SONSBEEK WELCOMES LAZYKING

T F G C Publishing

01 Albert Naasner

```
DDDD     UUU     SSSS
D    D   U   U   S    S
DDDD     U   U   SSSS
D        U   U   S
D        UUU     S
```

Popkultur in Düsseldorf e.V.

02 Open Studio

Base Design

Sander Vermeulen (design director)

Deep thought concepts, clear layouts, and sensitive typography: Brussels-based Sander Vermeulen is an independent graphic designer as well as Base Design's design director since 2009. Base's international agency network offers a variety of competencies, claiming to make the complex simple and the informative entertaining. In this interview, Vermeulen explains what design has to do with cycling, why brands are like humans, and what purified the logo.

Sander, you've worked at Base for about five years. You are an independent designer, why Base?
Whether it's with people from other domains or designers with different interests, it's great to work with people who can bring a fresh look or a certain savoir-faire to a project. Besides that, working at Base has given me the opportunity to work on projects with a more global scale, which in return allows you as a designer to reach a broader audience.

Base Design is a network of agencies in Brussels, Geneva, New York, and Santiago, working for big players like Adidas, Chanel, or Pantone. What is the studio culture like at Base?
We very much value the human aspect of our work: we don't want to design for designers, we want to design for people. And with people! As mentioned, collaboration is a key element in the creation process at Base. Moreover, I like to think we enjoy playing with codes and we're not afraid to challenge existing design habits and media. Nor are we afraid to make mistakes, because there's always something to learn from them.

On your own website* you compare your design process to cycling. What does "mental masochism" mean in your work?
Questioning your work, yourself, your work process, emotionally swinging back and forth between euphoria and feeling completely incompetent. Being ready to give it 300 percent, by starting over and over again until you can live with the result. It is tiring but at the same time very satisfying.

*www.iamsanderson.com

Base claims: "brands are like people." How can a logotype, a typeface, or colors be human?
It's much bigger than that. Brands today can surprise and delight, but they can just as easily betray and disappoint. The relationship we have with brands has become much more human. We no longer judge a brand solely based on how it looks but just as much on how it acts. Graphic elements can help you strengthen your brand identity, but it's the entire brand experience that will eventually define your brand image in the mind of your consumers. Brands today need to be honest and responsible. If you're going to talk the talk, you've got to walk the walk.

You are involved in a broad range of projects – from editorial design to web design to environmental projects. What does a logo have to look like today to function on various levels?
There are two important changes that have influenced the design of logos. Firstly, there's the rise of digital media, which has quickly brought on a new variety of formats and platforms. Besides the traditional logo used for stationery and other classic paper-applications, we've noticed a need for more compact versions of logos, such as monograms, for digital use. A second change links back to the "brands are like people" statement: the logo has become more purified. It no longer needs to tell the whole story, as the brand experience does this instead. We're also seeing less and less fixed baselines and more fluid storytelling, which allows brands to evolve over time (just like people do).

You are responsible for the new corporate design of Munich's Haus der Kunst, a museum housed in a building with a long and constantly changing history. How did you respond to the commission?
The original briefing focused on the open character of the museum, which introduces visitors with a wide variety of works, disciplines, information, and allows them to make their own associations. While working on the identity, we linked this to the idea of elasticity: the building, an icon of ideological power, becoming a cultural sherpa that guides visitors to "stretch their view".

As a former illustrator you also like to draw and paint. Why do you find Gerhard Richter fascinating?
I very much like his work. His constant process of trial and error is something I admire and can relate to. I also appreciate the dialogue between figurative and abstract, paint and photography, the beauty of color and the horror of paint being ripped apart. It is a battlefield of colors.

Why do designers necessarily love books, as you put it?
I think we live in fleeting times of brief moments and short-lived objects. It seems the book has somehow avoided this tendency for the temporary and will continue to do so in the future, with smaller print runs but nicer editions. The book as an object is becoming just as important as the content. When you are creating a book, you have the feeling you are creating something which will last a while, that will withstand the test of time. It's the designer's legacy.

German industrial designer Dieter Rams once said: "good design is as little design as possible." True?
It depends on which context you put that in, but in general it's certainly something I can relate to. The difficulty of minimal design is you don't have any extra elements to cover up any mistakes or imperfections. The design must shine in its simplicity. As John Maeda puts it in his book *The Laws of Simplicity*: "The best designers in the world squint when they look at something. They squint to see the forest from the trees – to find the right balance. Squint at the world. You will see more by seeing less".

HAUSD   E   RKUNST

HAUSD   E   RK   U   N   S   T

H   A   U   SDERKUNST

01 Base

223 Typo-Playful

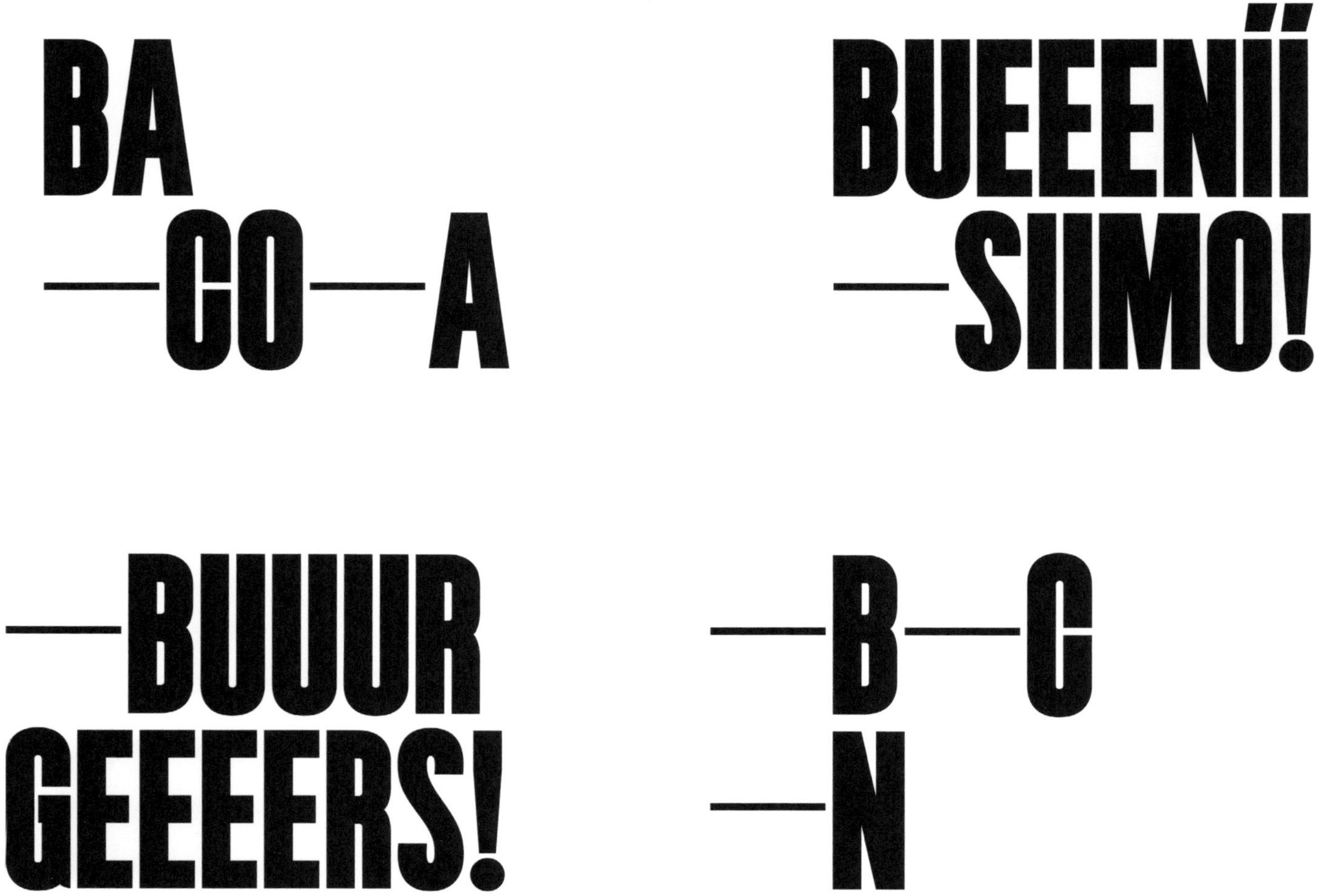

BA
—CO—A

BUEEENÏÏ
—SIIMO!

—BUUUR
GEEEERS!

—B—C
—N

01 TwoPoints.Net

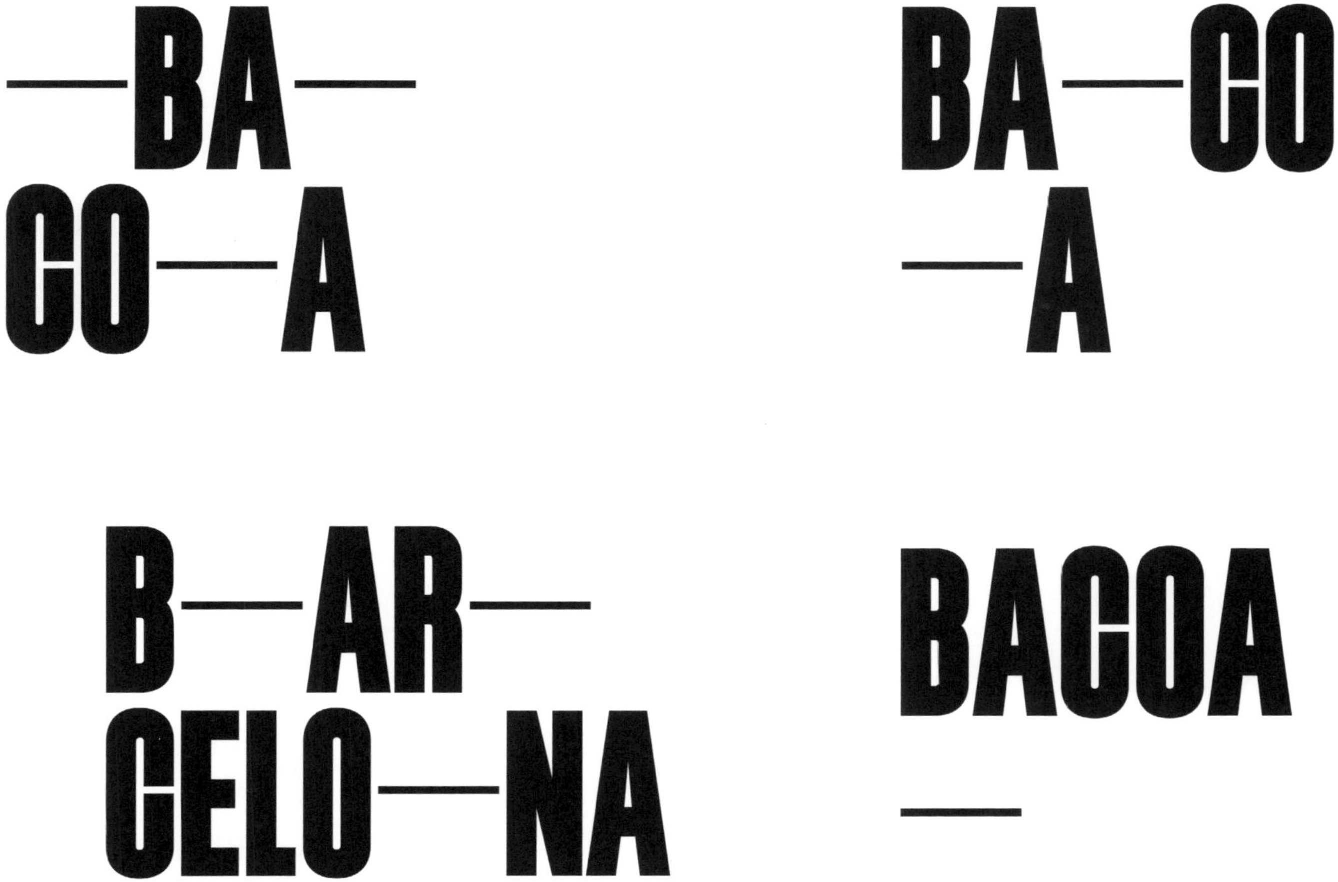

BA
CO—A

BA—CO
—A

B—AR
CELO—NA

BACOA
—

01 TwoPoints.Net

STREET CAMP

OCULTO

01 Jamie Mitchell

02 Morey Talmor

POLARIS

03 Intercity

04 Matt Le Gallez

FUTURE METHOD STUDIO

SLASH

01 Jamie Mitchell

02 Struggle inc.

GUT

CHIMA

03 Stefano Bracci

04 Floor 5

PAUL MORLEY

PIERO/BOANO

01 Dirk König

02 Federico Landini

POLA FOSTER

03 Manifiesto Futura

ALEKSANDER BRUNO

TOOT SWEET

04 Piotrek Chuchla

05 Ross Gunter

01 UVMV

CHRISTOPHER AMOTT

01 Bureau Lukas Haider

FOREVERNDECAY

02 Loic Sattler

PRIMAALA

03 Red Box Inc.

04 Nicklas Hultman

Doris & Doris

05 Vallée Duhamel

ECLECTIC

ECLECTIC ECLECTIC

01 Mind Design

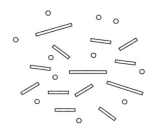

AGENT
AZUR

AGENT
AZUR

AGENT
AZUR

AGENT
AZUR

01 Bureau F

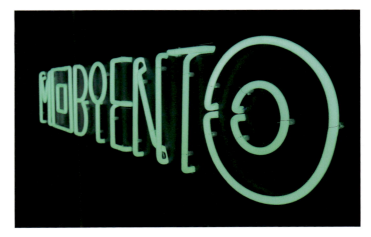

01 SNASK

02 George Popov

03 Haltenbanken

01 LLdesign

02 Faith

03 Stefano Bracci

01 STAHL R

02 Manifiesto Futura

03 Vier5

04 Trafik

HANNA UKURA

01 Dalston

ANTIQUERIST

02 Dirk König

ØLIVER

03 Akatre

04 Non-Format

INSTITUTE OF HARMLESS THINKING

05 Dirk König

01 Stefano Bracci

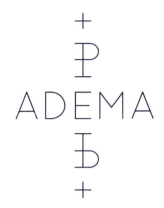

02 Studio AH-HA

03 100und1

PERMZ8

04 John Langdon

DAVVN

05 Floor 5

S A M ⊙⊙

06 Gianni Rossi

Typo-Playful 243

</ di. natives>   </ di. natives>   </ di. natives>   </ di. natives>

</ di. natives>   </ di. natives>   </ di. natives>   </ di. natives>

</ di. natives>   </ di. natives>

01 Raum Mannheim

Typo-Playful 245

01 Nohemi Dicuru

FASHION
GRAPHIC

02 Bureau Hardy Seiler

03 Wanja Ledowski

01 Pony Design Club

02 Studio Regular

03 Manifiesto Futura

04 Bleed

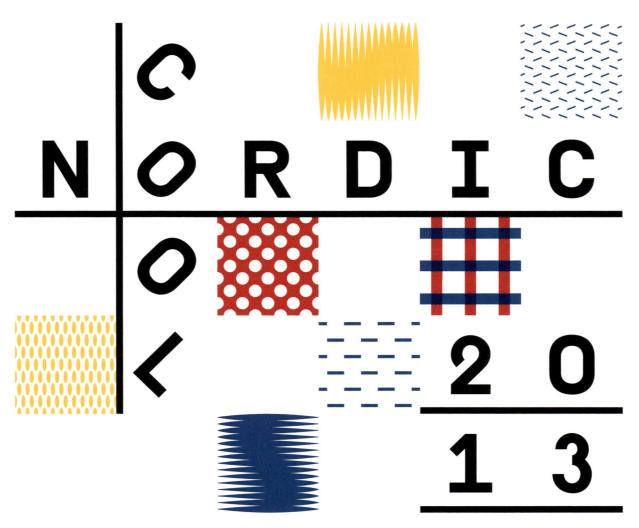

01 Kokoro & Moi

```
        K
    D   I
  T W E N
    E R
    L
```
01 büro uebele

```
B
-V
 -A
```
02 Fivethousand Fingers

```
B
 A
  S
   E
    M
     E
      N
|     T
PRESS———T
```
03 Trademark?

```
N
 O
  V
   E
    L
     T
      Y
```
04 Anagrama

01 BUREAU MALTE METAG

02 Richard Baird

03 Raum Mannheim

04 LA TIGRE

250 Typo-Playful

MA
RA
SO
MM
ER

01 Brogen Averill

STY
LI
STA

02 Making Waves

SYMPHONIE
ORCHESTER
DES
BAYERISCHEN
RUNDFUNKS

03 Bureau Mirko Borsche

L'Onde
Théâtre
Centre d'art

04 Akatre

Typo-Playful 251

01 Bureau Mirko Borsche

02 e-Types A/S

01 Richard Baird

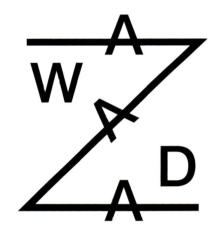

02 Jonathan Zawada

03 Studio Moross

04 Re-public

01 Eps51 Graphic Design Studio

02 Lee Goater

FESTSPILLENE I BERGEN

03 Anti

HET GELUID VAN ROTTERDAM

01 Ropp

02 Salutpublic

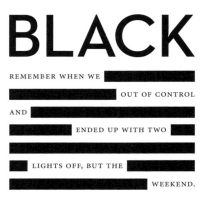

03 Anti

LA
DA
TCHA

M O N T A Ñ A

01 Fulguro

02 Francesc Moret

01 Ryan Feerer

02 Stefano Bracci

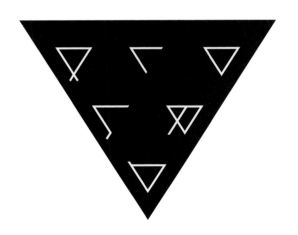

03 Manifiesto Futura

04 Kanardo

01 LLdesign

02 Mondbewohner

03 Mondbewohner

04 100und1

01 Albert Naasner

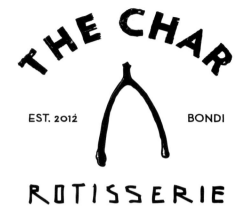

02 The National Grid

03 Kelly D. Williams

04 Anagrama

01 Struggle inc.

02 The National Grid

03 A-Side Studio

04 Albin Holmqvist

05 Nicklas Hultman

06 Quinta-Feira

01 Tobias Munk

02 Quinta-Feira

03 Albert Naasner

04 George Popov

05 Kanardo

01 Chragokyberneticks

02 Studio Moross

03 100und1

04 Alfredo Conrique

01 Alfredo Conrique

02 Alfredo Conrique

03 Via Grafik

04 Andrei Robu

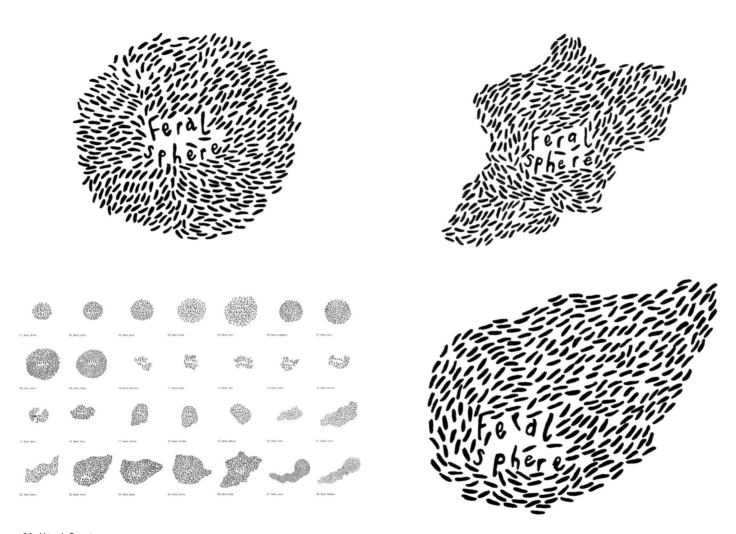

01 Mind Design

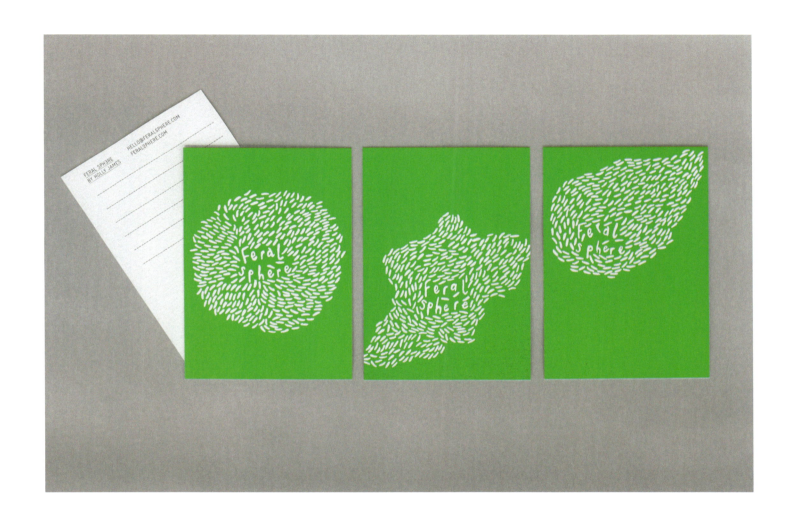

01 Mind Design

Kokoro

Teemu Suviala and Antti Hinkula (founders)

After separating from their former agency Syrup LLC in 2007, Teemu Suviala and Antti Hinkula founded the full-service creative agency Kokoro & Moi with a focus on strategies, identities, as well as interactive and graphic design. From their offices in Helsinki and New York City, the agency serves cities, commerce, and culture with clients such as American Institute of Architects, Nokia, Kennedy Center, Uniqlo, and Helsinki Design Week, to name but a few.
Suviala and Hinkula like turning to timeless ideas to create something new – a method reflected in the duo's name: while the word Kokoro is Japanese and means heart, mind, and soul, Moi is Finnish for hello and goodbye but also a wink to Norwegian celebrity chef Trond Moi.
The agency's striking visual language stands out in a world overloaded with messages. For instance, for the Brooklyn-based Dumbo Arts Center, Suviala and Hinkula used constructive elements from the area's surrounding bridges to create a tailor-made typeface, and for the annual Ihme art festival, the duo designed a logo in the shape of a piece of toast inscribed with mayonnaise.

Kokoro or Moi?
Moi!

Helsinki or New York?
Hel York

Black or white?
Billie Jean

Art or design?
Design

Circle or square?
Hip to be circle.

Historic or contemporary?
Contemporary

Work or play?
Play play play

Brain or heart?
Heart

Ketchup or mayonnaise?
Mayo. More mayo, please.

Cats or dogs?
Dogs

Form or function?
Form N' Function

Guns or roses?
Guns N' Roses

& Moi

Roses or tulips?
Tulips

Perfection or imperfection?
Imperfection

Questions or answers?
Apparently the latter.

Jeans or suit?
Well, there's a time for both – but never together, thank you.

Red or Blue?
Blue

Books or films?
Books and films

Mountains or ocean?
Mountains and ocean, close to each other. Yes, closer. Closer. That's good.

Analogue or digital?
Both in perfect harmony.

Dots or stripes?
Stripes

Bodoni or Helvetica?
Helvetica

Style or variety?
Variety

Concept or improvisation?
Improvisation concept

Money or love?
L-O-V-E

Baroque or Bauhaus?
Baroque

Fictive or real?
What is real? Therefore: fictive.

Secret or clearness?
It's a secret.

Modern or classic?
Always the latest classics.

Syrup or independence?
Absolutely independence

01 Kokoro & Moi

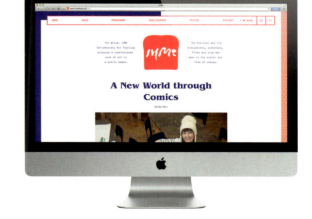

01 Kokoro & Moi

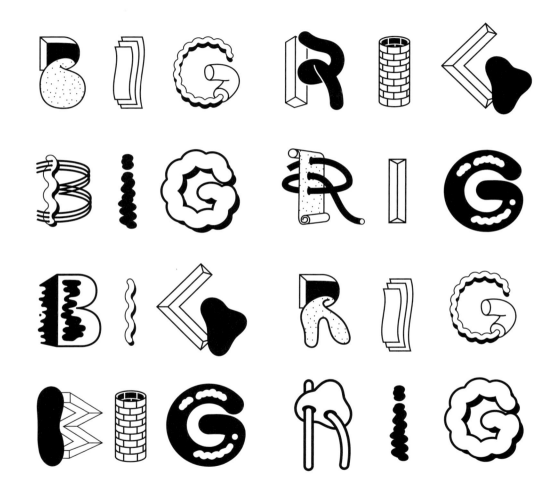

01 Zweizehn

01 Bravo Company

SIÂN DARLING

01 Rudi de Wet

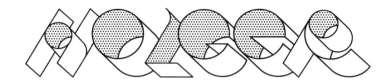

01 Hula + Hula Design

02 MASA

03 Brand New History?

04 Johan Thuresson

01 Sweyda

02 Tyrsa

03 Denis März

02 Andrei Robu

01 Sweyda

03 DTM_INC

Typo-Playful 275

01 Super Top Secret

02 Alfredo Conrique

03 Gitte Thrane

01 Double Standards

Typo-Playful 277

01 Rudi de Wet

02 Struggle inc.

03 Kelly D. Williams

04 Digitaluv

01 Irving & Co

02 Jordy van den Nieuwendijk

01 Modo

02 Simon Seidel

03 Andreas Neophytou

02 Karol Gadzala is YLLV

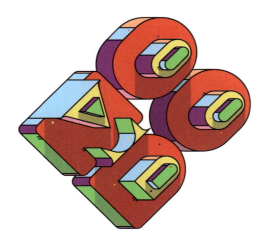

01 Modo

03 Acme Industries

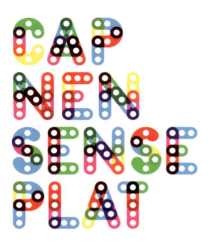

01 Torrents

02 Haigh + Martino

03 Escobas

04 Europa

01 Büro Destruct

02 Heydays

03 Heroes Design

01 Sasha Prood

01 Jon Kennedy

02 Sasha Prood

03 Toshikazu Nozaka

04 Jun Kaneko

05 Bold Stockholm

01 BOND CREATIVE AGENCY OY

01 hopa studio

CAPiTA

01 Tyler Quarles

SUITED CONCEPTS

02 Trapped in Suburbia

VERTIGE

03 HappyMess Studio

PRESTO

04 Via Grafik

NEW CUT!

05 Kokoro & Moi

06 Coup

01 Trapped in Suburbia

01 Pierre Vanni

02 Jonathan Zawada

03 ATTAK

04 Kokoro & Moi

01 Oblique

02 Sabina Keric

03 COMMUNE

04 Tomato

01 NNNNY

02 Dirk König

03 Walter Giordano

01 Aro

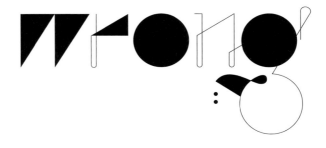

02 Federico Landini

03 Federico Landini

04 Anarchy Alchemy

01 Non-Format

02 Bureau Mirko Borsche

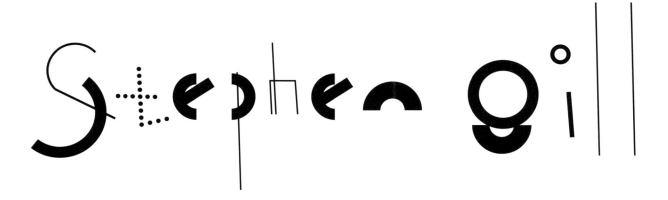

03 Non-Format

01 ZeCraft

02 OAT Creative Design Studio

03 Stitch Design Co.

04 BUREAU Mario Lombardo

01 Fivethousand Fingers

02 alessandridesign

HOFBURG WIEN

03 Tyrsa

04 Werklig

01 Anagrama

02 Fairchildesign

03 Alejandro Paul

04 Sergey Shapiro

05 Konstantinos Gargaletsos

06 erretres.

01 Anagrama

02 Haigh + Martino

03 Inkgraphix

04 Werklig

05 OAT Creative Design Studio

06 Inkgraphix

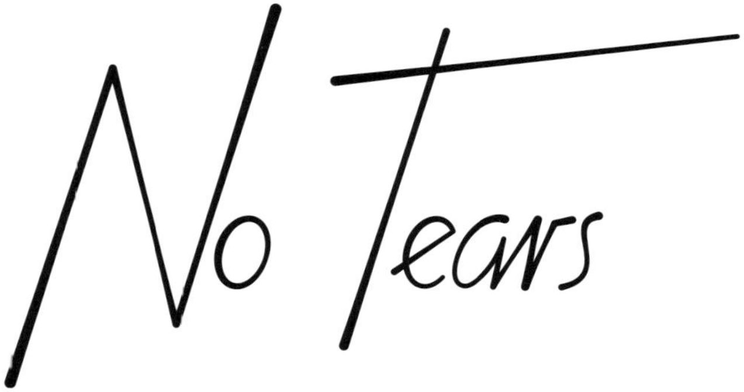

01 Dirk König

02 Gonzalo Rodriguez Gaspar

03 Brendan Prince

04 Andrei Robu

05 Ortografika

300 Script

01 Codefrisko

02 Sergey Shapiro

03 Peter Steffen

04 Aro

Script 301

01 Daniel Blik

salling

02 Maria Lyng

03 Inkgraphix

Trim tab

04 Pony Design Club

05 Noeeko

01 Atelier Dessert

02 Andrei Robu

03 Aro

04 La Tortillería

05 Maria Lyng

06 Aro

07 Christine Vallaure

01 SNASK

01 Andrew Woodhead

02 OAT Creative Design Studio

BROOKLYN EST. 2012

04 mgmt design

NORDIC TASTE

03 Quique Ollervides

05 Maria Lyng

01 Sergey Shapiro

02 GOOQX

03 IS Creative Studio

04 Studio Moross

05 Calligrapher Mami

01 Toben

02 Noeeko

03 100und1

04 Inkgraphix

05 La Tortillería

01 BMD Design

308 Script

01 BMD Design

01 BMD Design

01 BMD Design

01 BMD Design

312 Script

01 BMD Design

01 Sergey Shapiro

02 Tyler Quarles

03 Manifiesto Futura

01 Tyler Quarles

02 ilovedust

03 Aldo Lugo

04 21bis

01 Jon Contino

01 Anagrama

02 Ali Khorshidpour

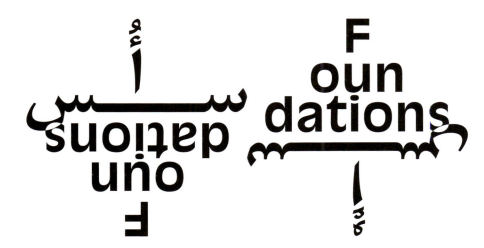

01 Eps51 Graphic Design Studio

02 Ali Khorshidpour

01 Eyal Baumert

01 Eyal Baumert

01 Yasuwo Miyamura

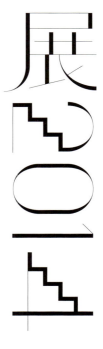

01 Foreign Policy Design Group

02 Yasuwo Miyamura

03 Non-Format

01 Yasuwo Miyamura

02 Jaemin Lee

03 Uji Design

04 Yasuwo Miyamura

01 Yasuwo Miyamura

02 Calligrapher Mami

03 Yasuwo Miyamura

01 Verena Michelitsch

02 Rickey Lindberg

03 Feed

04 Wanja Ledowski

01 Olsson Barbieri

01 Stier Royal

02 ROMstudio

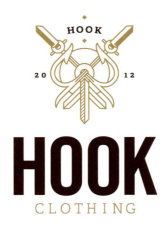

03 ROMstudio

04 Aro

01 Konstantinos Gargaletsos

02 [ˈændiː] Andrea Romano

03 Quique Ollervides

04 Milosz Klimek

01 Magpie Studio

02 Ryan Feerer

01 Ryan Feerer

02 De Jongens Ronner

01 Anti/Anti

02 Max-o-matic

03 Alen 'Type08' Pavlovic   04 Anti/Anti

01 Noeeko

02 ilovedust

01 Patrick Molnar

02 Chris Rubino

03 IS Creative Studio

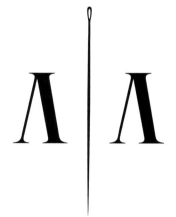

04 Kissmiklos

01 Bold Stockholm

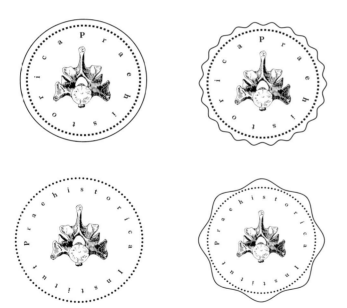

01 Zweizehn

01 HappyMess Studio

02 Yu Ping Chuang

03 alessandridesign

04 Mash

01 Shinpei Onishi

02 SWSP Design

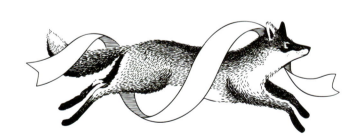

03 Anagrama

04 TARZAN+JANE

01 Meyer Miller Smith

02 OAT Creative Design Studio

03 One Design

01 Roxane Lagache

01 Conspiracy Studio

02 Chad Michael

03 Conspiracy Studio

04 310k

05 Live To Make

Emblem 341

01 Lange & Lange

02 Jaemin Lee

03 Gaetan Billault

01 Karolis Kosas

02 Csaba Bernáth

03 Anagrama

04 Andrei Robu

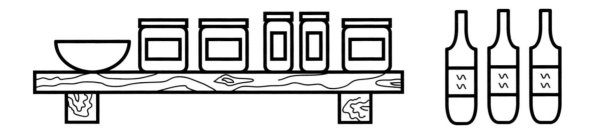

SERIAL GRILLER

EST 2013

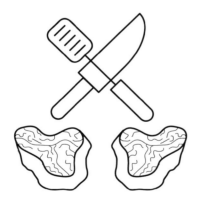

SERIAL GRILLER

EST 2013

01 CHRISTIANCONLH

02 Mash

01 Mikey Burton

01 High Tide

01 Funnel: Eric Kass

02 Metastazis.com

03 Metastazis.com

04 Chad Michael

01 Tobias Munk

02 Ludlow Kingsley

03 Gonzalo Rodriguez Gaspar

04 Manifiesto Futura

01 Calango

02 Kanardo

03 Andrei Robu

04 Chad Michael

01 Homework

02 Andreas Töpfer

03 Albert Naasner

04 Olsson Barbieri

01 Bergfest

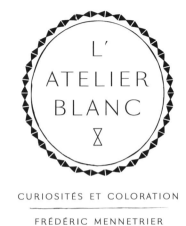

02 2Codefrisko

03 Csaba Bernáth

04 Noeeko

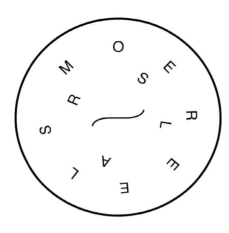

02 Live To Make

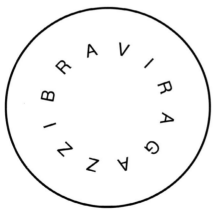

01 CHRISTIANCONLH

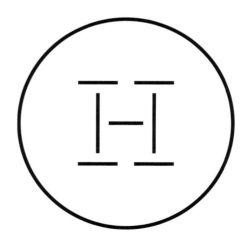

03 Ineo Designlab

352 Circle

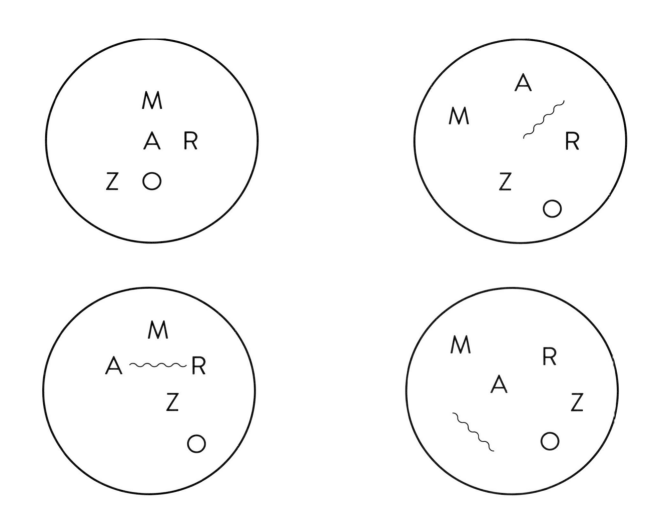

01 DAS.Graphiker

01 Mikey Burton

02 RUBÉN B

03 Andreas Klammt

04 Büro Glöwing

05 Via Grafik

06 Raum Mannheim

07 Jonathan Calugi

08 Jamie Mitchell

09 Alen 'Type08' Pavlovic

10 Gianmarco Magnani

01 Rob Angermuller

02 Conspiracy Studio

03 Albin Holmqvist

04 Áron Jancsó

05 Face

06 Andreas Klammt

07 Family

08 Bergfest

09 Laundry

10 cabina

01 busybuilding

02 BUREAU MALTE METAG

03 Aro

04 cabina

05 Alter

06 Bianca Dumitrascu

07 Face

08 SWSP Design

09 Jules Césure

10 Julianna Goodman

11 Andreas Klammt

12 Demetrio Mancini

13 brandmor

01 Deutsche & Japaner

02 Anna Magnussen

03 Black-Marmalade

04 Alen 'Type08' Pavlovic

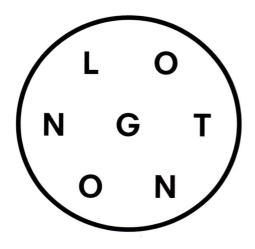

01 Longton

01 Longton

01 Bureau Mirko Borsche

360 Circle

50 JAHRE NATIONALTHEATER WIEDERERÖFFNUNG

01 Bureau Mirko Borsche

01 Chris Henley

02 High Tide

03 Clusta

04 BankerWessel

05 Calango

06 Bureau F

07 UNIT

08 Raum Mannheim

09 brandmor

10 cabina

11 Brogen Averill

12 Áron Jancsó

13 Calango

14 backyard 10

01 Mash

02 Federico Landini

03 Alltagspaparazzi

01 Simon Seidel

02 Derek A. Friday

03 Bleed

04 &Larry

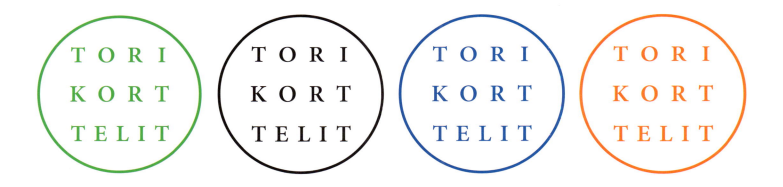

01 Kokoro & Moi

02 Théo Gennitsakis

03 Büro Destruct

01 Tyler Quarles

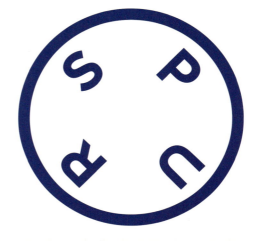

02 ACRE

03 Mikey Burton

04 MoreSleep

366 Circle

01 Edhv

02 Base

03 Mutabor Design

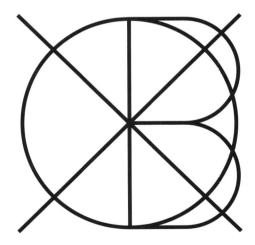

04 Csaba Bernáth

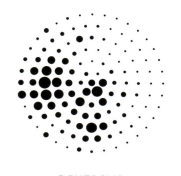

DEUTSCHE
STIMMKLINIK

02 Mutabor Design

01 Roxane Lagache

LUKAS
STROCIAK
RETOUCHING.

03 Noeeko

01 Gytz Studio

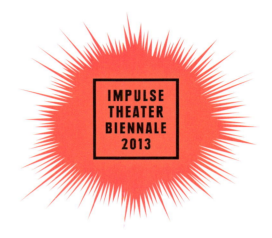

02 Fons Hickmann m23

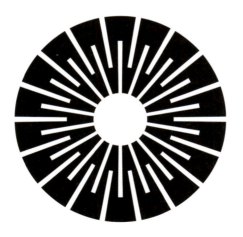

03 Berger & Föhr

Circle 369

01 Ludlow Kingsley

02 Ryan Feerer

03 OAT Creative Design Studio

04 Studio Regular

01 IS Creative Studio

02 Paper and Tea

03 Albert Naasner

04 Cutts Creative

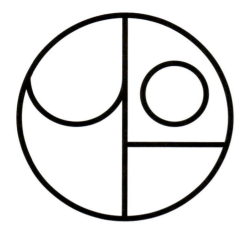

01 Bedow Creative

AMERICAN HOMEMADE BAKERY

SURFBOARDS

MFG.

01 Pierre de Belgique

02 Peter Steffen

Circle 373

01 Pony Design Club

02 Jonathan Sandridge

03 Filmgraphik

04 Evelin Kasikov

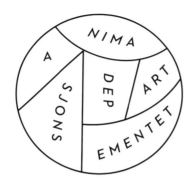

01 Olsson Barbieri

02 Bleed

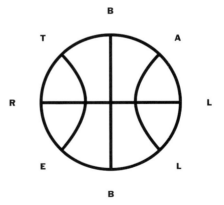

03 Albert Naasner

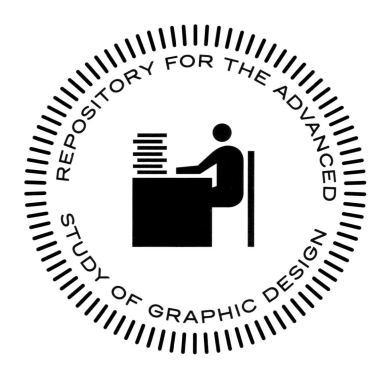
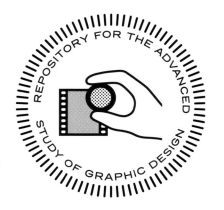
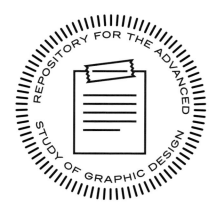

01 Ian Lynam Design

01 CHRISTIANCONLH

02 Rob Angermuller

03 Longton

04 Milosz Klimek

01 21bis

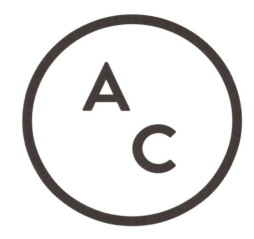

02 Ludlow Kingsley

03 Grzegorz Sołowiński

04 Mutabor Design

01 HappyMess Studio

02 COMMUNE

Circle 379

Address Index

##

10 Associates United Kingdom
www.10associates.co.uk
Page 111

21bis Netherlands
www.21bis.nl
Pages 315, 378

44flavours Germany
www.44flavours.de
Pages 138, 139, 144, 145

100 und 1 Austria
www.100und1.com
Pages 175, 243, 258, 262, 307

310k Netherlands
www.310k.nl
Pages 173, 341

903 Creative United States
www.903creative.com
Page 13

['ændi:] Andrea Romano Germany
www.ro-nanoandrea.de
Pages 159, 196, 329

&Larry Singapore
www.andlarry.com
Pages 31, 62, 364

##

Acre Singapore
www.acre.sg
Pages 10, 26, 91, 135, 366

Acme Industries Romania
www.acmeindustries.ro
Pages 64, 204, 281

Aim Studio Germany
www.iamaim.com
Page 73

Akatre France
www.akatre.com
Pages 30, 242, 251

Akinori Oishi Japan
www.aki-air.com
Pages 138, 144

Albert Naasner Germany
www.naasner.com
Pages 26, 31, 143, 158, 225, 259, 261, 350, 371, 375

Albin Holmqvist Sweden
www.albinholmqvist.com
Pages 260, 355

Aldo Lugo Mexico
www.aldolugo.com
Pages 157, 315

Alejandro Paul Argentina
www.sudtipos.com
Page 298

Alen 'Type08' Pavlovic Croatia
www.dribbble.com/type08
Pages 110, 332, 354, 357

Alessandridesign Austria
www.alessandri-design.at
Pages 164, 166, 207, 297, 337

Alex Trochut Spain
www.alextrochut.com
Pages 189, 199, 200

Alfredo Conrique Mexico
www.heypogo.com
Pages 157, 262, 263, 276

Ali Khorshidpour
Pages 318, 319

Alltagspaparazzi Germany
www.alltagspaparazzi.de
Page 363

Alter Australia
www.alter.com.au
Pages 24, 60, 61, 356

Anagrama Mexico
www.anagrama.com
Pages 11, 27, 46, 47, 57, 185, 198, 249, 259, 298, 299, 318, 338, 343

Anarchy Alchemy Germany
www.anarchyalchemy.com
Pages 160, 294

Andrea Münch Switzerland
www.andreamuench.com
Pages 67, 123

Andreas Klammt | 53,5 Germany
www.andreasklammt.de
Pages 165, 354, 355, 356

Andreas Neophytou
United States
www.work.andreasneophytou.com
Pages 178, 280

Andreas Töpfer Germany
www.andreastoepfer.blogspot.com
Page 350

André Beato Portugal
www.andrebeato.com
Pages 114, 198

Andrei Robu Thailand
www.andreirobu.com
Pages 201, 263, 275, 300, 303, 343, 349

Andrew Woodhead France
www.andrewwoodhead.com
Pages 28, 305

Anna Magnussen Denmark
www.annamagnussen.dk
Pages 159, 357

Anna-OM-line Spain
www.anna-OM-line.com
Page 204

Anonimo Studio Venezuela
www.titanpost.tv
Page 185

Anti Norway
www.anti.as
Pages 41, 54, 254, 255

Anti / Anti United States
www.antiantinyc.com
Pages 185, 332

Antonio Ladrillo Spain
www.antonioladrillo.com
Page 187

Aristu & Co Spain
www.aristu.com
Page 30

Áron Jancsó Hungary
www.aronjancso.com
Pages 355, 362

Aro | Christian Schupp
Germany
www.aroone.de
Pages 18, 128, 195, 208, 216, 294, 301, 303, 328, 356

A-Side Studio United Kingdom
www.a-sidestudio.co.uk
Pages 29, 260

Atelier Dessert Switzerland
www.dessert.ch
Pages 173, 303

Atelier télescopique France
www.ateliertelescopique.com
Page 87

Attak Netherlands
www.attakweb.com
Page 291

B

Backyard 10 Germany
www.backyard10.com
Pages 114, 362

BankerWessel Sweden
www.bankerwessel.com
Pages 78, 362

Base Switzerland
www.basedesign.com
Pages 209, 228, 367

Bedow Creative Sweden
www.bedow.se
Page 372

Berger & Föhr United States
www.bergerfohr.com
Pages 21, 167, 369

Bergfest Germany
www.bergfest.at
Pages 110, 147, 351, 355

Bianca Dumitrascu Romania
www.biancadumitrascu.com
Page 356

Black-Marmalade United States
www.black-marmalade.com
Page 357

Bleed Norway
www.bleed.com
Pages 27, 123, 247, 364, 375

Bmd Design France
www.bmddesign.fr
Pages 308, 309, 310, 311, 312, 313

Bold Stockholm Sweden
www.boldstockholm.se
Pages 94, 285, 335

Bo Lundberg Illustration Ab
Sweden
www.bolundberg.com
Page 209

Bond Creative Agency Oy
Finland
www.bond.fi
Page 286

Booth Canada
www.wearebooth.com
Page 21

Braca Burazeri Serbia
www.bracaburazeri.com
Page 156

Branded | Studio for visual communication Austria
www.wearebranded.at
Page 117

Brandmor Romania
www.brandmor.ro
Pages 19, 174, 186, 356, 362

Brand New History? Germany
www.brandnewhistory.net
Page 273

Bravo Company Singapore
www.bravo-company.info
Page 271

Brendan Prince United States
www.brendanprince.com
Pages 201, 300

Brogen Averill New Zealand
www.brogenaverill.com
Pages 12, 251, 362

Bunch United Kingdom
www.bunchdesign.com
Pages 18, 32, 33, 108

Bureau Bleen Germany
www.bureaubleen.com
Page 48

Bureau F / Fabienne Feltus
Austria
www.ffabienne.com
Pages 238, 362

Bureau Hardy Seiler Germany
www.hardyseiler.de
Page 246

Bureau Lukas Haider Austria
www.lukashaider.com
Pages 19, 43, 49, 199, 236

Bureau Malte Metag
Germany
www.maltemetag.de
Pages 250, 356

Bureau Mario Lombardo
Germany
www.mariolombardo.com
Pages 26, 176, 188, 196, 296

Bureau Mirko Borsche Germany
www.mirkoborsche.com
Pages 27, 176, 185, 187, 251, 252, 295, 360, 361

Büro Destruct Switzerland
www.burodestruct.net
Pages 8, 129, 283, 365

Büro Glöwing Germany
www.gloewing.de
Pages 56, 354

Büro Uebele Germany
www.uebele.com
Page 249

Busybuilding Greece
www.busybuilding.com
Page 356

C

Cabina Argentina
www.espaciocabina.com.ar
Pages 160, 180, 181, 195, 355, 356, 362

Calango Netherlands
www.calango.nl
Pages 349, 362

Calligrapher Mami Japan
www.66mami66.com
Pages 306, 325

Canefantasma Studio United Kingdom
www.canefantasma.com
Page 177

Carsten Giese | Studio Regular Germany
www.studio-regular.com
Pages 247, 370

Cerotreees United Kingdom
www.cerotreees.com
Page 123

Chad Michael United States
www.chadmichaelstudio.com
Pages 12, 119, 136, 137, 203, 211, 341, 347, 349

Chragokyberneticks Switzerland
www.chragokyberneticks.ch
Pages 145, 164, 262

Chris Henley United Kingdom
www.goodandbrave.co.uk
Page 362

Chris Rubino United States
www.chrisrubino.com
Pages 55, 334

Christianconlh Italy
www.cargocollective.com/christianconlh
Pages 38, 344, 352, 377

Christine Vallaure Germany
www.christinevallaure.com
Pages 218, 303

Christian Rothenhagen / graphics & illustration Germany
www.christianrothenhagen.com
Pages 108, 113

Ciau.Aa.Kee Spain
www.clauaskee.com
Pages 43, 74

Cindy T. Mai United States
www.cindytm.com
Pages 139, 155

Clase Bcn Spain
www.clasebcn.com
Page 48

Cless Spain
www.cless.info
Page 153

Clusta United Kingdom
www.clusta.com
Page 362

Codefrisko Belgium
www.codefrisko.be
Pages 13, 43, 108, 195, 301, 351

Côme de Bouchony France
www.comedebouchony.com
Pages 186, 222

Commune Japan
www.commune-inc.jp
Pages 292, 379

Conspiracy Studio Spain
www.conspiracystudio.com
Pages 128, 208, 341, 355

Cooee Graphic Design Netherlands
www.cooee.nl
Page 100

Core60 Romania
www.core60.com
Pages 38, 76

Coup Netherlands
www.coup.nl
Pages 40, 74, 289

Csaba Bernáth Hungary
www.csababernath.com
Pages 160, 206, 343, 351, 367

Cursor Design Studio Greece
www.cursor.gr
Page 10

Cutts Creative Australia
www.cuttscreative.tumblr.com
Pages 156, 205, 371

D

Dadada Studio Lithuania
www.dadadastudio.eu
Pages 57, 113, 215

Dainippon Type Organization Japan
www.dainippon.type.org
Page 65

Dalston Sweden
www.dalston.se
Page 242

Daniel Blik Hungary
www.blikdani.com
Pages 213, 302

Daniele Politini United States
www.danielepolitini.com
Page 28

Das Buro Netherlands
www.dasburo.nl
Page 116

Das.Graphiker Mexico
www.dasgraphiker.com
Pages 27, 353

Dave Sedgwick United Kingdom
www.studiodbd.com
Pages 88, 89

David Büsser Switzerland
www.davidbuesser.com
Pages 56, 125, 126

Deanne Cheuk United States
www.deannecheuk.com
Page 178

De Jongens Ronner Netherlands
www.dejongensronner.nl
Pages 135, 214, 331

Demetrio Mancini Italy
www.demetriomancini.it
Page 356

Denham Netherlands
www.denhamthejeanmaker.com
Page 161

Denis März Germany
www.denis-maerz.de
Pages 196, 198, 274

Dennis Herzog Germany
www.derherzog.com
Pages 135, 198

Derek A. Friday United States
www.instagram.com/derekfriday
Page 364

DesignJune France
www.designjune.com
Pages 153, 156, 165

Desres Design Group Germany
www.desres.de
Page 180

Deutsche & Japaner Germany
www.deutscheundjapaner.com
Pages 72, 186, 357

Di-Da Spain
www.di-da.com
Pages 41, 145

Digitaluv Denmark
www.digitaluv.com
Page 278

Dimomedia Lab Italy
www.dimomedia.com
Page 29

Dirk Büchsenschütz Germany
www.dbuechsenschuetz.de
Page 12

Dirk König Germany
www.dirkkoenig.com
Pages 234, 242, 293, 300

Double Standards Germany
www.doublestandards.net
Pages 90, 277

Down With Design United Kingdom
www.downwithdesign.com
Page 114

Drach P. Claude France
www.cargocollective.com/pclaudedrach
Page 216

Dtm_Inc Netherlands
www.behance.net/dtm_inc
Page 275

Dr. Morbito Mexico
www.drmorbito.com.mx
Page 154

E

Edgar Bąk Poland
www.edgarbak.info
Page 38

Edhv Netherlands
www.edhv.nl
Pages 218, 367

Eduardo Vidales Mexico
www.eduarvidales.tk
Page 140

El Solitario Spain
www.elsolitariomc.com
Pages 162, 163

Emil Hartvig Denmark
www.eha.dk
Page 86

Empk Brazil
www.empk.net
Page 8

Eps51 Graphic Design Studio Germany
www.eps51.com
Pages 30, 126, 254, 319

Erik Kiesewetter | Constance United States
www.weareconstance.org
Pages 39, 49

Erretres. Spain
www.erretres.com
Pages 188, 298

Escobas Mexico
www.behance.net/el_escobas5df1
Pages 212, 282

Espluga+Associates Spain
www.espluga.net
Page 188

Estudio Soma Argentina
www.estudiosoma.com.ar
Page 209

E-Types A/S Denmark
www.e-types.com
Pages 72, 252

Europa United Kingdom
www.europaeuropa.co.uk
Page 282

Evelin Kasikov United Kingdom
www.evelinkasikov.com
Page 374

Eyal Baumert Israel
www.eyalbaumert.com
Pages 320, 321

F

Fabio Milito Design Italy
www.fabiomilito.com
Page 79

Face Mexico
www.designbyface.com
Pages 76, 122, 170, 188, 355, 356

Fairchildesign United States
www.fairchildesign.com
Page 298

Faith Canada
www.faith.ca
Page 240

Family United Kingdom
www.stu.dio-family.com
Pages 183, 355

Federico Landini Italy
www.idependonme.com
Pages 234, 294, 363

Feed Canada
www.studiofeed.ca
Pages 9, 326

Filmgraphik Germany
www.filmgraphik.com
Pages 8, 187, 374

Finsta Sweden
www.finstafari.com
Page 156

Fivethousand Fingers Canada
www.fivethousandfingers.net
Pages 31, 43, 185, 249, 297

Floor 5 Germany
www.flcor5.de
Pages 9, 110, 233, 243

Fons Hickmann m23 Germany
www.fonshickmann.com
Pages 69, 127, 202, 369

Fontan 2 Bulgaria
www.fontan2.com
Pages 41, 66, 72, 124

Foreign Policy Design Group Singapore
www.foreignpolicydesign.com
Page 323

Förm Germany
www.foerm.net
Page 157

Francesc Moret Spain
www.francescmoret.com
Page 256

Francisco Elias Portugal
www.franciscoelias.com
Page 80

Franck Juncker | fjopus7 Canada
www.fjopus7.com
Pages 74, 132

Frank Aloi Australia
www.frankaloi.com.au
Page 13

Friedrich Santana Lamego Brazil
www.ntera.com.br
Page 170

Fulguro | Yves Fidalgo & Cédric Decroux Switzerland
www.fulguro.ch
Pages 70, 71, 102, 220, 256

Full Color Canvas United States
www.fullcolorcanvas.com
Pages 110, 197

Funnel: Eric Kass United States
www.funnel.tv
Pages 136, 205, 347

Fuzzco United States
www.fuzzco.com
Pages 10, 39, 41, 115, 211

G

Gaetan Billault United Kingdom
www.gaetan-billault.com
Page 342

Genauso.und.anders Germany
www.genausoundanders.com
Page 189

George Popov Germany/Russia
www.georgepopov.com
Pages 67, 144, 239, 261

Gianmarco Magnani Peru
www.silencetv.com
Pages 42, 354

Gianni Rossi Italy
www.giannirossi.net
Pages 67, 243

Gitte Thrane Denmark
www.gittethrane.dk
Page 276

Glenn Garriock Germany
www.garriock.com
Page 202

Gonzalo Rodriguez Gaspar Germany
www.dribbble.com/GRG
Pages 11, 158, 300, 348

Gooqx Germany
www.gooqx.com
Pages 64, 209, 306

GrandArmy United States
www.grand-army.com
Page 113

Graphinya Ukraine
www.graphinya.com
Pages 75, 212

Gravit Art Germany
www.gravitart.com
Pages 124, 189

Grzegorz Sołowiński Poland
www.solowinski.com
Page 378

Gytz Studio Denmark
www.gytzstudio.com
Page 369

H

Haigh + Martino United States
www.haighandmartino.com
Pages 282, 299

Haltenbanken Norway
www.haltenbanken.com
Page 239

HappyMess Studio France
www.happymess.fr
Pages 42, 49, 66, 109, 146, 222, 289, 337, 379

Heroes Design – Piotr Buczkowski Poland
www.heroesdesign.com
Pages 174, 176, 283

Heydays Norway
www.heydays.no
Pages 30, 283

High Tide United States
www.hightidenyc.com
Pages 9, 346, 362

Homework Denmark
www.homework.dk
Pages 183, 185, 186, 188, 350

Hopa Studio Poland
www.hopastudio.com
Pages 48, 288

Hort Germany
www.hort.org.uk
Pages 141, 221, 223

Hovard Design United States
www.hovarddesign.com
Pages 208, 211

Hovercraft Studio United States
www.hovercraftstudio.com
Pages 19, 130

Hüfner Design Germany
www.huefner-design.de
Page 43

Hugo Hoppmann Germany
www.hugohoppmann.com
Page 52

Hula + Hula Design Mexico
www.hulahula.com.mx
Pages 138, 158, 273

Hype Type Studio United States
www.hypetype.co.uk
Pages 79, 115

I

Ian Lynam Design Japan
www.ianlynam.com
Page 376

Identity Estonia
www.identity.ee
Page 202

Ilovedust United Kingdom
www.ilovedust.com
Pages 315, 333

Image now Ireland
www.imagenow.ie
Page 112

Indyvisuals United Kingdom
www.indyvisuals.net
Pages 118, 119, 199

Ineo Designlab Denmark
www.ineo.dk
Page 352

Inkgraphix Sweden
www.inkgraphix.com
Pages 59, 299, 302, 307

Intercity United Kingdom
www.intercitystudio.com
Pages 10, 91, 232

Inventaire Switzerland
www.inventaire.ch
Page 134

Irving & Co United Kingdom
www.irvingandco.com
Pages 215, 279

Is Creative Studio Peru
www.iscreativestudio.com
Pages 78, 147, 306, 334, 371

J

Jacknife Canada
www.jacknifedesign.com
Pages 106, 107

Jacques et Brigitte Switzerland
www.jacquesetbrigitte.com
Page 157

Jaemin Lee South Korea
www.studiofnt.com
Pages 34, 342

Jamie Mitchell Australia
www.jamiemitchell.com.au
Pages 232, 233, 354

Jan Moucha / Work-N-Roll Czech Republic
www.work-n-roll.com
Page 139

Jeremy Pruitt | Thinkmule United States
www.thinkmule.com
Pages 131, 134, 157, 166

Jochen Kuckuck Germany
www.jochenkuckuck.de
Pages 56, 111, 137, 142

Johan Thuresson Sweden
www.johanthuresson.se
Pages 99, 273

John Langdon United States
www.johnlangdon.net
Page 243

Jonas Ganz Switzerland
www.jonasganz.ch
Page 80

Jonathan Calugi Italy
www.happyloverstown.eu
Pages 167, 169, 354

Jonathan Sandridge United States
www.jonathansandridge.com
Page 374

Jonathan Zawada United States
www.zawada.com.au
Pages 253, 291

Jon Contino United States
www.joncontino.com
Pages 150, 151, 199, 316

Jon Kennedy Czech Republic
www.jonkennedy.co.uk
Page 285

Jono Garrett Germany
www.jonogarrett.com
Pages 16, 137

Jordy van den Nieuwendijk Netherlands
www.jordyvandennieuwendijk.nl
Page 279

José Design Netherlands
www.jose-design.nl
Pages 77, 79

Josiah Jost Canada
www.siahdesign.com
Pages 112, 185, 206

Jules Césure Belgium
www.jules-cesure.com
Page 356

Julian Hrankov Germany
www.julianhrankov.com
Page 119

Julianna Goodman / Design + Art Direction (J G / D + A D) United States
www.juliennagoodman.com
Pages 177, 356

Jun Kaneko Japan
www.junkaneko.co.jp
Page 285

K

Kanardo France
www.kanardo.com
Pages 131, 257, 261, 349

Karol Gadzala is Yllv Germany
www.matcadesign.com
Page 281

Karolis Kosas United States
www.karoliskosas.com
Page 343

Kasper Gram Denmark
www.kaspergram.com
Pages 14, 15

Kelly D. Williams United States
www.artwontsaveyou.com
Pages 259, 278

Kissmiklos Hungary
www.kissmiklos.com
Pages 74, 177, 178, 179, 180, 184, 189, 194, 200, 208, 334

Kokoro & Moi Finland
www.kokoromoi.com
Pages 11, 24, 26, 48, 51, 248, 268, 269, 289, 291, 365

Kommerz Netherlands
www.kommerz.nl
Pages 92, 93

Konstantinos Gargaletsos United Kingdom
www.konstantinosgargaletsos.co.uk
Pages 30, 31, 42, 298, 329

Kursiv | Peter Graabaek Denmark
www.kursiv.dk
Pages 50, 104

L

Lab-2 Germany
www.lab-2.net
Pages 58

Laboratoř Czech Republic
www.laboratory.cz
Page 29

Lange & Lange Poland
www.langeandlange.com
Pages 10, 213, 342

La Tigre Italy
www.latigre.net
Page 250

La Tortillería Mexico
www.latortilleria.com
Pages 128, 207, 303, 307

Laundry United States
www.laundrymat.tv
Pages 156, 178, 355

Lee Goater United Kingdom
www.leegoater.com
Page 254

Linnea Blixt Sweden
www.linneablixt.com
Page 203

Live To Make United States
www.livetomake.com
Pages 8, 77, 168, 172, 204, 341, 352

Lldesign Italy
www.lldesign.it
Pages 222, 240, 258

Loic Sattler France
www.lysergid.com
Page 236

Longton Australia
www.longtondesign.com
Pages 55, 184, 358, 359, 377

Ludlow Kingsley United States
www.ludlowkingsley.com
Pages 348, 370, 378

Lundgren+Lindqvist Sweden
www.lundgrenlindqvist.se
Pages 184, 224

M

Made by Molloy United States
www.madebymolloy.com
Page 11

Mads Burcharth Denmark
www.mabu.dk
Page 12

Magpie Studio United Kingdom
www.magpie-studio.com
Pages 21, 199, 330

Making Waves Norway
www.makingwaves.no
Page 251

Mañana Communication Germany
www.maniana-design.de
Page 173

Manifiesto Futura Mexico
www.mfutura.mx
Pages 30, 184, 185, 234, 241, 247, 257, 314, 348

Maniackers Design | Masayuki Sato Japan
www.mksd.jp
Pages 139, 206

Maria Lyng France
www.marialyng.dk
Pages 302, 303, 305

Martin Silvestre France
www.martinsilvestre.com
Page 57

Masa Venezuela
www.masa.com.ve
Pages 52, 140, 273

Mash Australia
www.mashdesign.com.au
Pages 129, 337, 344, 363

Matt Le Gallez United Kingdom
www.mattlegallez.com
Pages 53, 232

Matt Vergotis Australia
www.verg.com.au
Page 215

Matt W. Moore United States
www.mwmgraphics.com
Page 52

Maximilian Baud Germany
www.umsinn.com
Pages 118, 184

Max-o-matic Spain
www.maxomatic.net
Pages 167, 332

Mehdi Saeedi Islamic Republic of Iran
www.mehdisaeedi.com
Page 171

Metastazis.com France
www.metastazis.com
Page 347

Meyer Miller Smith Germany
www.meyermillersmith.com
Page 339

Mgmt Design United States
www.mgmtdesign.com
Page 305

Mikey Burton United States
www.mikeyburton.com
Pages 345, 354, 366

Milosz Klimek Poland
www.miloszklimek.com
Pages 77, 172, 329, 377

Mind Design United Kingdom
www.minddesign.co.uk
Pages 237, 264, 265

Minigram Studio für Markendesign Germany
www.minigram.de
Pages 176, 181

Mm75 Design Switzerland
www.mm75design.ch
Page 211

Modo Venezuela
www.modovisual.com
Pages 155, 280, 281

Moker Netherlands
www.mokerontwerp.nl
Page 201

Mondbewohner Germany
www.mondbewohner.com
Pages 122, 258

MoreSleep GmbH & Co. KG Germany
www.moresleep.net
Pages 56, 366

Morey Talmor Israel
www.moreytalmor.com
Page 232

Mr. Brown – creative boutique Poland
www.mrbrown.pl
Page 205

Mr. Magenta Spain
www.mrmagenta.net
Pages 55, 72, 73

Mr Walczuk Poland
www.mr_walczuk.com
Pages 54, 76, 127

Mutabor Design GmbH Germany
www.mutabor.de
Pages 96, 97, 105, 367, 368, 378

N

Name and Name Taiwan, Province of China
www.nameandname.com
Page 64

Neeser & Müller Switzerland
www.neesermueller.ch
Page 51

Nicholaus Jamieson United States
www.nicjamieson.com
Page 143

Nicklas Hultman Sweden
www.valentin.se
Pages 236, 260

Noeeko – Design Studio Poland
www.noeeko.com
Pages 111, 123, 146, 166, 302, 307, 333, 351, 368

Nohemi Dicuru Spain
www.nohemidicuru.com
www.fashiongraphic.com
Pages 86, 246

Non-Format United States
www.non-format.com
Pages 122, 242, 295, 323

Núria Vila Spain
www.nuriavila.net
Page 224

O

Oat Creative Design Studio United States
www.oatcreative.com
Pages 296, 299, 305, 339, 370

Oblique Belgium
www.oblq.be
Page 292

Olivier Charland Canada
www.oliviercharland.com
Pages 56, 132

Olsson Barbieri Norway
www.olssonbarbieri.com
Pages 6, 7, 207, 210, 327, 350, 375

Omochi Japan
Page 167

One Design New Zealand
www.onedesign.co.nz
Pages 25, 339

Onlab Germany
www.onlab.ch
Pages 51, 194

Open Studio Germany
www.weareopenstudio.de
Pages 68, 225

Ortografika Poland
www.ortografika.eu
Page 300

P

Paper and Tea Germany
www.paperandtea.com
Page 371

Partly Sunny United States
www.partly-sunny.com
Page 118

Passport United Kingdom
www.wearepassport.com
Pages 36, 37, 182

Patrick Molnar Germany
www.patrickmolnar.de
Pages 133, 334

Paul Coors United States
www.paulcoors.com
Pages 89, 160

Pedro Paulino Brazil
www.pedropaulino.com
Pages 24, 67, 81, 188

Peter Steffen United Kingdom
www.petersteffen.com
Pages 301, 373

Pierpaolo Scarpato Italy
Page 134

Pierre de Belgique France
www.pierredebelgique.fr
Page 373

Pierre Vanni France
www.pierrevanni.tumblr.com
Page 291

Piotrek Chuchla Poland
www.piotrekchuchla.com
Page 234

PolkaGrafik United States
www.polkagrafik.com
Page 212

Pony Design Club Netherlands
www.ponydesignclub.nl
Pages 50, 195, 221, 247, 302, 374

Por Amor al Arte Spain
www.poramoralarte.es
Page 194

Post Typography United States
www.posttypography.com
Page 73

Q

Qoop | Design & Kommunikation Germany
www.hello-qoop.com
Pages 24, 57

Quinta-Feira Brazil
www.quinta-feira.org
Pages 101, 103, 260, 261

Quique Ollervides Mexico
www.ollervides.com
Pages 305, 329

R

R2 Design Portugal
www.r2design.pt
Pages 53, 132, 197

Raum Mannheim Germany
www.raum-mannheim.com
Pages 75, 245, 250, 354, 362

Red Box Inc. Canada
www.creativeredbox.com
Page 236

Re-public Denmark
www.re-public.com
Pages 28, 253

Richard Baird Czech Republic
www.richardbaird.co.uk
Pages 75, 250, 253

Rickey Lindberg Denmark
www.rickeylindberg.dk
Pages 109, 125, 213, 326

Rob Angermuller United States
www.angermuller.info
Pages 79, 171, 355, 377

Roberto Funke Germany
www.robertofunke.de
Page 216

Roman Kirichenko Russian Federation
www.kirichenkodesign.com
Page 112

Rom Studio Mexico
www.romstudio.com.mx
Page 328

Ropp Netherlands
www.ropp.nl
Page 255

Ross Gunter United Kingdom
www.rossgunter.com
Pages 194, 234

Roxane Lagache France
www.roxanelagache.com
Pages 214, 340, 368

Roy Smith United Kingdom
www.roysmithdesign.com
Pages 109, 116

Rubén B Spain
www.rubenb.info
Pages 137, 177, 354

Rudi de Wet South Africa
www.rudidewet.com
Pages 272, 278

Rüdiger Götz Germany
www.kw43.de
Page 197

Ryan Feerer United States
www.ryanfeerer.com
Pages 135, 136, 257, 330, 331, 370

S

Sabina Keric Germany
www.sabinakeric.de
Page 292

Salon91 Germany
www.salon91.de
Pages 118, 188

Salutpublic Belgium
www.salutpublic.be
Pages 75, 95, 255

Sammy Stein France
www.sammystein.fr
Page 153

Sanscolor Norway
www.sanscolor.com
Pages 189, 192, 193

Sasha Prood United States
www.sashaprood.com
Pages 128, 284, 285

Sawdust United Kingdom
www.madebysawdust.co.uk
Page 171

Sellout Industries Germany
www.sellout-industries.org
Pages 142, 154

Sergey Shapiro Russian Federation
www.sergeyshapiro.ru
Pages 298, 301, 306, 314

Shinpei Onishi Japan
www.shinpeionishi.com
Pages 159, 338

Sid Lee Canada
www.sidlee.com
Pages 20, 22, 84, 85

Signers Germany
www.signers.de
Pages 54, 115

Simon Seidel Germany
www.simonseidel.com
Pages 280, 364

Smart Heart Russian Federation
www.smart-heart.ru
Page 98

Snask Sweden
www.snask.com
Pages 239, 304

Sociodesign United Kingdom
www.sociodesign.co.uk
Page 183

Stahl R Germany
www.stahl-r.com
Page 241

Stefano Bracci Italy
www.avantbras.com
Pages 173, 233, 240, 243, 257

Steven Bonner United Kingdom
www.stevenbonner.com
Page 108

Stier Royal Germany
www.facebook.com/Stier.Royal
Pages 203, 328

Stitch Design Co. United States
www.stitchdesignco.com
Pages 112, 205, 206, 214, 296

Struggle inc. United States
www.struggleinc.com
Pages 142, 143, 233, 260, 278

Studio Ah-ha Portugal
www.studioahha.com
Pages 212, 216, 217, 243

Studio No. 10 Sweden
www.no10.se
Page 49

Studio Moross United Kingdom
www.studiomoross.com
Pages 11, 139, 253, 262, 306

Studio Output United Kingdom
www.studio-output.com
Page 187

Sunday Vision Japan
www.sunday-vision.com
Page 129

Super Top Secret United States
www.wearetopsecret.com
Page 276

Surface Germany
www.surfacegrafik.de
Page 109

Swear Words Australia
www.swearwords.com.au
Pages 29, 81, 122, 123, 132, 187

Sweyda United States
www.sweyda.com
Pages 274, 275

Swsp Design Germany
www.schatzdesign.de
Pages 338, 356

T

Tabas France
www.tabas.fr
Page 124

Taeko Isu | Nnnny Japan
www.nnr-ny.jp
Pages 129, 293

Tarzan + Jane Switzerland
www.tarzanundjane.ch
Page 338

Teacake Design United Kingdom
www.teacakedesign.com
Pages 165, 204, 215

The National Grid Australia
www.thenationalgrid.com.au
Pages 119, 131, 134, 203, 259, 260

Théo Gennitsakis France
www.theogennitsakis.com
Page 365

The Simple Society Germany
www.thesimplesociety.com
Page 57

Thonik Netherlands
www.thonik.nl
Pages 120, 224

Till Paukstat Germany
www.tilloky.de
Page 28

Tim Bjørn Denmark
www.madebytim.com
Page 168

Tim Boelaars Netherlands
www.timboelaars.nl
Pages 77, 168, 171

Tnop Thailand
www.tnop.com
Page 89

Toben Australia
www.toben.com.au
Page 307

Tobias Munk Denmark
www.tobiasmunk.com
Pages 56, 171, 261, 348

Tomato United Kingdom
www.tomato.co.uk
Pages 79, 217, 292

Tomato Kosir Slovenia
www.tomatokosir.com
Pages 127, 220

Tom Grant United Kingdom
www.tom-grant.co.uk
Page 186

Tom Hingston Studio United Kingdom
www.hingston.net
Page 196

Torrents Spain
www.torrents.info
Pages 28, 282

Toshikazu Nozaka Japan
www.toshikazu-nozaka.com
Pages 152, 285

Trademark? United States
www.trademark-trademark.com
Pages 29, 113, 147, 249

Trafik France
www.lavitrinedetrafik.fr
Page 241

Trapped in Suburbia Netherlands
www.trappedinsuburbia.com
Pages 289, 290

Triboro Design United States
www.triborodesign.com
Page 168

Tridente Brand Firm Mexico
www.tridente.mx
Page 170

Tropenelektronik Germany
www.tropenelektronik.de
Page 115

TwoPoints.Net Spain
www.twopoints.net
Pages 230, 231

Two Times Elliott United Kingdom
www.2×elliott.co.uk
Pages 76, 78, 79

Tyler Quarles Canada
www.tylerquarles.com
Pages 9, 289, 314, 315, 366

Typejockeys Austria
www.typejockeys.com
Page 165

Tyrsa France
www.tyrsa.fr
Pages 13, 152, 198, 200, 274, 297

U

Uji Design Japan
www.ujidesign.com
Page 324

Unfolded Switzerland
www.unfolded.ch
Page 184

Unit United Kingdom
www.weareunit.com
Pages 125, 362

Uvmv Poland
www.uv-warsaw.com
Page 235

V

Vallée Duhamel Canada
www.valleeduhamel.com
Pages 53, 236

Verena Michelitsch United States
www.verenamichelitsch.com
Pages 57, 216, 326

Vértice Comunicación Mexico
www.verticecom.com
Pages 13, 136

Via Grafik Germany
www.vgrfk.com
Pages 263, 289, 354

Vier5 France
www.vier5.de
Pages 158, 241

Vonsung United Kingdom
www.vonsung.com
Pages 170, 181

W

Walter Giordano Italy
www.waltergiordano.com
Pages 29, 293

Wanja Ledowski France
www.wanjaledowski.com
Pages 31, 184, 197, 246, 326

Werklig Finland
www.werklig.com
Pages 124, 186, 297, 299

Y

Yasuwo Miyamura Japan
www.bouse.jp
Pages 322, 323, 324, 325

Yotam Bezalel Studio Israel
www.yotam-bezalel.com
Page 213

Yu Ping Chuang United States
www.yuping.prosite.com
Page 337

Z

ZeCraft France
www.zecraft.com
Pages 30, 186, 187, 189, 296

Zek Slovenia
www.zek.si
Pages 11, 111, 219

Zeroipocrisia Italy
www.zeroipocrisia.com
Page 186

Zumquadrat – Visuelle Kommunikation Germany
www.zumquadrat.com
Pages 125, 194

Zweizehn Germany
www.zweizehn.com
Pages 175, 270, 336

Work Index

06.01 Olsson Barbieri
◊ Beverages & Spirits
$ Moestue Grape Selections

07.01 Olsson Barbieri
◊ Beverages & Spirits
$ Moestue Grape Selections

08.01 Büro Destruct

08.02 Filmgraphik
◊ Film Production
$ Kings & Queens Filmproduktion

08.03 Live To Make
◊ Corporate & Business
$ Straw & Gold

08.04 Empk
◊ Furniture design
$ Sergio Fahrer

09.01 High Tide
• Danny Miller
◊ Lifestyle
$ Paperless Post

09.02 Tyler Quarles
◊ Media
$ Edward Foord & Company

09.03 Feed
◊ Bar
$ Rufus Rockhead

09.04 Floor 5
◊ Corporate & Business
$ R&S Hotelbetriebsgesellschaft

10.01 Fuzzco
◊ Fashion & Lifestyle
$ Candlefish

10.02 Acre
◊ Food, Beverage, Fashion, Hair salon
$ Pact

10.03 Intercity
◊ Corporate & Business
$ The Academy

10.04 Lange & Lange
◊ Branding
$ Lous clothes

10.05 Acre
◊ Food & Beverage
$ Yardstick Coffee

10.06 Cursor Design Studio
◊ Food & Beverage
$ S 'il Vous Plait

11.01 Made by Molloy
◊ Business
$ Nomad

11.02 Zek
◊ Sport & Lifestyle
$ Musguard

11.03 Studio Moross
◊ Music
$ Xenomania Recordings

11.04 Gonzalo Rodriguez Gaspar
◊ Media, art
$ Wolfhouse Productions

11.05 Kokoro & Moi
◊ Public
$ Kota

11.06 Anagrama
$ Nordic House

12.01 Chad Michael
◊ Business, Real Estate
$ Empire Real Estate

12.02 Brogen Averill
◊ Corporate and Business
$ The Talent Factory

12.03 Mads Burcharth
◊ Film production
$ Prmry

12.04 Dirk Büchsenschütz
◊ Corporate & Business, Music, Culture
$ Timo Bader

13.01 Codefrisko
◊ Food
$ Gazzetta—Caffè & Deli

13.02 Frank Aloi
◊ Food & Beverage
$ Charlie's Espresso Bar

13.03 Tyrsa
• Alexis Taieb
◊ Restaurant
$ Barbershop Paris

13.04 Vértice Comunicación
• Juan Carlos Alatorre, Miriam Ramos
◊ Food & Beverages
$ La Flor de Córdoba

14.01 Kasper Gram
◊ Food & beverage
$ Karma Sushi

15.01 Kasper Gram
◊ Food & Beverage
$ Karma Sushi

16.01 Jono Garrett
◊ Corporate & Business, Design
$ Frida von Fuchs

18.01 Bunch
◊ Corporate & Business
$ Willow Tree

18.02 903 Creative
• Aaron Gibson
◊ Veterinary, animal care
$ DogServices

18.03 Aro | Christian Schupp
◊ Music
$ Soundkonstrukt

19.01 Brandmor
• Mako Lehel Mor
◊ Food
$ Gradyva

19.02 Hovercraft Studio
◊ Hospitality
$ Ce John Real Estate Development

19.03 Bureau Lukas Haider
◊ Corporate & Business
$ Tresorfabrik

20.01 Sid Lee
• Philippe Meunier, Simon Chénier-Gauvreau, Aldine
$ Chartier

21.01 Magpie Studio
◊ Interior design
$ Baldwin Harris

21.02 Berger & Föhr
◊ Food & Beverage
$ Jack Rabbit Hill Farm

21.03 Booth
• Christian & Allegra Poschmann
◊ Hospitality
$ The Secret Garden Inn

22.01 Sid Lee
• Philippe Meunier, Simon Chénier-Gauvreau, Aldine
$ Blue Goose

24.01 Pedro Paulino
◊ Food & Beverage
$ Flavio Tupinamba, Tiago Otani, Fernando Pereira

24.02 Kokoro & Moi
◊ Technology
$ AddSearch

24.03 Qoop | Design & Kommunikation
◊ Distribution, Coporate & Business
$ Hood Distribution

24.04 Alter
◊ Hospitality
$ Viva Brazil

25.01 One Design
◊ Hospitality
$ Michael & Annette Dearth

26.01 Albert Naasner
◊ Fashion
$ Masomaso

26.02 Kokoro & Moi
◊ Cultural
$ Finnish Cultural Institute for Benelux

26.03 Bureau Mario Lombardo
◊ Art & Culture
$ Logo for the gallery exchange Berlin Paris

26.04 Acre
◊ Food & Beverage
$ Marco Marco

27.01 Bureau Mirko Borsche
◊ Food & Beverage
$ Bartu & Spitzenberger

27.02 Das.Graphiker
◊ Fashion & Lifestyle

27.03 Anagrama
◊ Checklist

27.04 Bleed
◊ Fashion & Lifestyle
$ Tom Wood Jewellery

28.01 Till Paukstat
◊ Fashion & Lifestyle, Magazine & Editorial
$ Monday Publishing

28.02 Torrents
• David Torrents, Silvia Míguez
◊ Cultural
$ Liniazero edicions

28.03 Re-public
• Thomas Braestrup
◊ Corporate & Business
$ Relate

28.04 Daniele Politini
◊ Cultural
$ The city of Florence

28.05 Andrew Woodhead
◊ Food & Beverage
$ The Sunken Chip

29.01 Laboratoř
• Petr Babák
◊ Cultural Institution
$ Amu

29.02 Swear Words
◊ Food & Beverage
$ Yomg

29.03 Dimomedia Lab
• Massimo Sirelli
◊ Music
$ I Lucchettino

29.04 Walter Giordano
• Proemotional
◊ Fashion & Lyfestyle, Editorial
$ Ovvio Magazine

29.05 Trademark?
◊ Media, Games & Technology
$ Gekko

29.06 A-Side Studio
◊ Cultural
$ Miracle Theatre

30.01 Aristu & Co
◊ Fashion
$ Tatiana Queiroz

30.02 Manifiesto Futura
◊ Food & Beverage
$ Doméstico

30.03 Konstantinos Gargaletsos
◊ Food & Beverage
$ W Verbier

30.04 Eps51 Graphic Design Studio
◊ Cultural
$ Ngbk Berlin

30.05 Akatre
◊ Akatre
◊ Cultural
$ Courtesy

30.06 ZeCraft
◊ Fashion, Design, & Publishing
$ Tzenkoff

30.07 Heydays
◊ Food & Beverage, hospitality
$ Bolivar

31.01 Fivethousand Fingers
◊ Music
$ Dear Rouge

31.02 Albert Naasner
◊ Art & Music

31.03 Wanja Ledowski
◊ Art, Cultural
$ J-a-d

31.04 &Larry
◊ Fashion & Lifestyle
$ Plush

31.05 Konstantinos Gargaletsos
◊ Food & Beverage,
$ W Verbier

32.01 Bunch
◊ Corporate & Business
$ Nosive Strukture

33.01 Bunch
◊ Corporate & Business
$ Nosive Strukture

34.01 Jaemin Lee
• Jaemin Lee, Heesun Kim, Woogyung Geel
◊ Fashion & Lifestyle
$ Twl

36.01 Passport
◊ Design
$ Laand

37.01 Passport
- ◊ Design
- $ Laand

38.01 Christianconlh
- ◊ Design
- • Personal
- ◊ Fashion & Lifestyle
- $ Bravi Ragazzi Shop

38.02 Core60
- ◊ Art
- $ Center for Visual Artists, Greensboro

38.03 Edgar Bąk
- ◊ Art
- $ Photomonth in Krakow

39.01 Fuzzco
- ◊ Corporate & Business
- $ Terra Mare Conservation

39.02 Erik Kiesewetter | Constance
- ◊ Art,
- $ Constance

40.01 Coup
- ◊ Cultural
- $ P/////akt

41.01 Di-Da
- • Gotzon Garaizabal, Joseba Attard
- ◊ Cultural Institution
- $ Aek

41.02 Fontan 2
- ◊ Corporate & Business
- $ Short Bio

41.03 Fuzzco
- ◊ Corporate & Business
- $ Lunch and Recess

41.04 Anti
- ◊ Sport, Corporate
- $ Birkebeinerrennet

42.01 HappyMess Studio
- • Mothi Limbu
- ◊ Design

42.02 Gianmarco Magnani
- ◊ Music, Film
- $ Personal

42.03 Konstantinos Gargaletsos
- ◊ Art
- $ Le Meridien

43.01 Hüfner Design
- • Tim Hüfner
- ◊ Design
- $ Hüfner Design

43.02 Fivethousand Fingers
- ◊ Art
- $ Black Visual Archive

43.03 Codefrisko
- ◊ Photography
- $ L+M Studio

43.04 Bureau Lukas Haider
- ◊ Music & Art
- $ Self-initiated

43.05 Ciau.As.Kee
- • Clau.as.kee
- ◊ Corporate & Business

46.01 Anagrama
- ◊ Food & Beverage
- $ Xoclad

47.01 Anagrama
- ◊ Food & Beverage
- $ Xoclad

48.01 Clase Bcn
- ◊ University
- $ Universitat Pompeu Fabra Barcelona

48.02 Hopa studio
- • Marcin Paściak
- ◊ Corporate & Business
- $ Billennium

48.03 Kokoro & Moi
- ◊ Cutural
- $ International Design Foundation

48.04 Bureau Bleen
- ◊ Corporate & Business
- $ Content & Container

49.01 Studio No. 10
- • Björn Carlsson
- ◊ Fashion & Lifestyle
- $ Dead Stock Creations

49.02 HappyMess Studio
- • Mothi Limbu
- ◊ Cultural
- $ Ldn Dancing

49.03 Bureau Lukas Haider
- ◊ Cultural
- $ Steo Forward

49.04 Erik Kiesewetter | Constance
- ◊ Cultural, Arts Guidebook
- $ City of New Orleans

50.01 Kursiv | Peter Graabaek
- ◊ Corperate & Business
- $ European Holiday Home Association

50.02 Pony Design Club
- ◊ Corporate & Business
- $ Bob van der Vlist

51.01 Kokoro & Moi
- ◊ Cultural
- $ Dumbo Arts Center

51.02 Onlab
- • Thibaud Tissot
- ◊ Cultural Institution
- $ Musée des beaux-arts Le Locle

51.03 Neeser & Müller
- ◊ Corporate Design
- $ Zia Textilatelier

52.01 Masa
- ◊ Artist & Music
- $ Royal Dust

52.02 Matt W. Moore
- ◊ Furniture, Business
- $ Core Deco

52.03 Hugo Hoppmann
- ◊ Music
- $ Cologne Sessions

53.01 Vallée Duhamel
- ◊ Cultural
- $ MassivArt

53.02 Matt Le Gallez
- ◊ Design
- $ Show Us Your Type

53.03 R2 Design
- • Lizá Ramalho, Artur Rebelo, assisted by José Maria Cunha
- ◊ Visual Identity
- $ Joaquim Portela Arquitectos

54.01 Mr Walczuk
- ◊ Fashion & Lifestyle
- $ Anna Kamkina

54.02 Signers
- • Pierre Enorm Exner – Signers

54.03 Anti
- ◊ Sport, Corporate
- $ Birkebeinerrennet

55.01 Mr. Magenta
- ◊ Music Band, Hip Hop, Music
- $ Garcha

55.02 Chris Rubino
- ◊ Television
- $ Hbo

55.03 Longton
- ◊ Design
- $ Czyk

56.01 Büro Glöwing
- ◊ Design
- $ Büro Glöwing

56.02 Tobias Munk
- $ Klub Far

56.03 David Büsser
- ◊ Corporate, Business & Design, Craft
- $ Bertschinger Innenausbau

56.04 Olivier Charland
- ◊ Design
- $ Land

56.05 Jochen Kuckuck
- ◊ Fashion & Lifestyle
- $ Frontlineshop.com

56.06 MoreSleep GmbH & Co. KG
- ◊ Corporate & Business
- $ MoreSleep

57.01 The Simple Society
- ◊ Fashion & Lifestyle, Cosmetics
- $ Oak Berlin

57.02 Martin Silvestre
- ◊ Art
- $ It's Numbered

57.03 Verena Michelitsch
- ◊ Jewelry, Fashion & Lifestyle
- $ Bb Jewelry

57.04 Qoop | Design & Kommunikation
- ◊ Lifestyle & Corporate
- $ Eden

57.05 Dadada studio
- ◊ Food & Beverages
- $ Le Butcher

57.06 Anagrama
- $ Valentto

58.01 Lab-2
- ◊ Design
- $ Lab2

59.01 Inkgraphix
- ◊ Art
- $ Fraktalfabriken

60.01 Alter
- ◊ Art
- $ Ten Cubed

61.01 Alter
- ◊ Art
- $ Ten Cubed

62.01 &Larry
- ◊ Art
- $ 2902 Gallery

64.01 Gooqx
- ◊ Art & Lifestyle
- $ Toykio

64.02 Name and Name
- • Ian Perkins, Matthew Gill, Andrew Poyiadgi, Steven Ackroyd
- ◊ Music
- $ My Little Party

64.03 Acme Industries
- • Paramon Dițu
- ◊ Cultural
- $ Vatra Pavilion Romania Milano 2015

65.01 Dainippon Type Organization
- ◊ Book title & Label
- $ Neo-logue inc.

66.01 Fontan 2
- ◊ Art
- $ Fontan 2

66.02 HappyMess Studio
- • Mothi Limbu
- ◊ Fashion, Kids
- $ Small Store

67.01 Andrea Münch
- ◊ Corporate & Business
- $ Raffaele Calzoni, créateurs d'architectures

67.02 George Popov
- ◊ Corporate & Business
- $ Themes for Great Cities

67.03 Gianni Rossi
- ◊ Cultural
- $ K3 Kurzfilm Festival

67.04 Pedro Paulino
- • Pedro Paulino
- ◊ Fashin & Lifestyle
- $ Enrico Benetti, Barbara Thomaz

68.01 Open Studio
- ◊ Design & Architecture
- $ Open Studio & Büro Steinhoff

69.01 Fons Hickmann m23
- ◊ Cultural
- $ Semperoper Dresden
- $ Theater und Philharmonie Essen

70.01 Fulguro | Yves Fidalgo & Cédric Decroux
- ◊ Cultural
- $ Epfl Lausanne

71.01 Fulguro | Yves Fidalgo & Cédric Decroux
- ◊ Health
- $ Hôpital Riviera-Chablais

72.01 Fontan 2
- ◊ Art
- $ Fontan 2

72.02 E-Types A/S
- ◊ Cultural
- $ The National Museum of Denmark

72.03 Deutsche & Japaner
- ◊ Music
- $ Blng Blng – blngblng.biz

72.04 Mr. Magenta
- ◊ Brand & Fashion
- $ Yo! clothing

• Designer name, if not identical with studio name   ◊ Category $ Client   © Credits

73.01 Mr. Magenta
◊ Music, Dj
$ Jesus Daniel Uscategui A.K.A Dj Folk

73.02 AIM Studio
• Christian Dueckminor
◊ Music, Art, Corporate & Business
$ Fiva

73.03 Post Typography
◊ Cultural
$ Maryland Institute College of Art

74.01 Kissmiklos
◊ Design
$ LuxDelux Studio

74.02 Franck Juncker | fjopus7
◊ Art
$ Fjopus7

74.03 Coup
◊ Art
$ Apice for Artists

74.04 Ciau.As.Kee
• Clau.as.kee
◊ Cultural Institution

75.01 Raum Mannheim
◊ Fashion & Lifestyle
$ Studio Masslos

75.02 Salutpublic
◊ Architecture
$ L'escaut

75.03 Richard Baird
◊ Interior Design
$ Alyssa M. Wieske

75.04 Graphinya
◊ Corporation & Business
$ Interior Lab. Store

76.01 Mr Walczuk
◊ Corporate & Business
$ Good Idea

76.02 Core60
◊ Corporate & Business
$ John Conrad / Conrad Companies

76.03 Two Times Elliott
◊ Design
$ Cord

76.04 Face
◊ Architecture
$ Guzve

77.01 Live To Make
◊ App
$ Golden Eagle

77.02 Tim Boelaars
$ Tim Boelaars

77.03 Milosz Klimek
◊ Logo design
$ Personal Identity

77.04 José Design
◊ Interactive Design, Art Direction, Motion, 3D, & Audio / Visual
$ Michael Novia

78.01 BankerWessel
• Jonas Banker, Ida Wessel
◊ Corporate & Business
$ Alessandro Ripellino Arkitekter

78.02 IS Creative Studio
◊ Art
$ Les Paradis Artificiels

78.03 Two Times Elliott
• Borheh
◊ Architecture
$ Borheh
• Fashion
$ Odmé Paris

79.01 Hype Type Studio
◊ Sport
$ Jordan Brand

79.02 Tomato
• Dylan Kendle
◊ Fashion & Lifestyle
$ Wrag Wrap

79.03 José Design
◊ Fashion, Accessories
$ Hongi

79.04 Rob Angermuller
◊ Coporate & Business
$ TechGrayscale

79.05 Fabio Milito Design
◊ Design
$ Fabio Milito Design

79.06 Two Times Elliott
◊ Interior Design
$ Daniel Hopwood

80.01 Jonas Ganz
◊ Design, Lamps, Light Objects
$ Kando, Felix Mosiman

80.02 Francisco Elias
◊ Architecture & Desgin
$ Ap.Art

81.01 Swear Words
◊ Furniture
$ Engrain

81.02 Pedro Paulino
◊ Corporate & Business
$ João Conrado e Gabriel Ceravolo

84.01 Sid Lee
◊ Philippe Meunier, Simon Chénier-Gauvreau, Aldine
$ Adc

85.01 Sid Lee
• Philippe Meunier, Simon Chénier-Gauvreau, Aldine
$ Adc

86.01 Emil Hartvig
◊ Recreation
$ PingOut

86.02 Nohemi Dicuru
• Music
$ Monzter. David Rondon & Dj Trujillo

87.01 Atelier télescopique
◊ Corporate & Business
$ Serre Numérique

88.01 Dave Sedgwick
◊ Culture
$ TwentyTwentyTwo

89.01 Dave Sedgwick
◊ Culture
$ TwentyTwentyTwo

89.02 Tnop
◊ Design
$ Tnop Design

89.03 Paul Coors
◊ Music
$ Helado Negro / Asthmatic Kitty Records

89.04 Dave Sedgwick
◊ Culture
$ TwentyTwentyTwo

90.01 Double Standards
◊ Corporate & Business
$ Echtwald

91.01 Acre
◊ Fashion & Lifestyle
$ Matter

91.02 Intercity
◊ Cultural Institution
$ I-Dat / Cheltenham Festivals

92.01 Kommerz
◊ Private Business, Education
$ Vakmanstad / Henk Oosterling

93.01 Kommerz
◊ Private Business, Education
$ Vakmanstad / Henk Oosterling

94.01 Bold Stockholm
◊ Cultural Institution
$ Swedish History Museum

95.01 Salutpublic
◊ Architecture
$ Dethier Architecture

96.01 Mutabor Design GmbH
◊ Corporate & Business, Chemistry
$ Clariant AG / Switzerland

97.01 Mutabor Design GmbH
◊ Corporate & Business, Chemistry
$ Clariant AG / Switzerland

98.01 Smart Heart
◊ Culture, Event branding, Mass Events, Ball
$ Ministry of sport, tourism and youth policy of Krasnoyarsk territory

99.01 Johan Thuresson
◊ Cultural
$ Musikaliska

100.01 Cooee Graphic Design
◊ Visual Identity
$ Gnp+

101.01 Quinta-Feira
◊ Corporate
$ Embyá

102.01 Fulguro | Yves Fidalgo & Cédric Decroux
◊ Art, Theatre, Dance
$ Théâtre Sévelin 36

103.01 Quinta-Feira
◊ Cultural Institution
$ Travessias

104.01 Kursiv | Peter Graabaek
◊ Art
$ Form:lab Research Cluster, The Royal Danish Academy of Fine Arts

105.01 Mutabor Design GmbH
◊ Hospitality
$ Weissenhaus Grand Village Resort

106.01 Jacknife
• Adam MacLean
◊ Music Event
$ Redbull

107.01 Jacknife
• Adam MacLean
◊ Music Event
$ Redbull

108.01 Bunch
◊ Fashion & Lifestyle
$ Borna & Fils

108.02 Steven Bonner
◊ Food & Beverage
$ Wimbledon Brewery

108.03 Codefrisko
◊ Design
$ June's

108.04 Christian Rothenhagen / graphics & illustration
◊ Corporate & Business
$ Lindgrün / Standard Petroleum

109.01 HappyMess Studio
• Mothi Limbu
◊ Cultural
$ Ldn Club / Bar / Label

109.02 Surface
◊ Cultural
$ Goethe-Universität Frankfurt am Main, Historisches Seminar

109.03 Rickey Lindberg
◊ Corporate & Business
$ Nathan Byrne

109.04 Roy Smith
◊ Design
$ Roadrunner

110.01 Floor 5
◊ Food & Beverage
$ Pets Deli

110.02 Bergfest
• Ari Bolk, Jens Uwe Meyer
◊ Fashion & Lifestyle
$ Ludwig Schröder 1825

110.03 Alen 'Type08' Pavlovic
• Alen Pavlovic
◊ Corporate & Business
$ Pride Legal

110.04 Full Color Canvas
• Jarrod Bryan
◊ Fashion & Lifestyle
$ Parker Dusseau

111.01 Jochen Kuckuck
◊ Corporate & Business
$ Xl1 Designkollektiv

111.02 10 Associates
- Jill Peel, James Bornshin
◊ Business
$ Ashwood House

111.03 Zek
◊ Sport, Bike, Fixed Gear, Community, Repair Shop
$ Muslauf, Musverks

111.04 Noeeko – Design Studio
◊ Fashion
$ Enemies

112.01 Roman Kirichenko
◊ Food & Beverage
$ Safari bar

112.02 Stitch Design Co.
◊ Design
• Sadie Mitchell

112.03 Josiah Jost
◊ Corporate & Business
$ Hummingbird

112.04 Image now
• David Torpey
◊ Food & Beverage
$ Peter McKenna

113.01 GrandArmy
◊ Corporate & Business
$ LionTree

113.02 Dadada studio
◊ Fashion & Lifestyle
$ Client who makes sweaters from alpaca wool

113.03 Trademark?
◊ Media, Games, Technology
$ Harvest

113.04 Christian Rothenhagen / graphics & illustration
◊ Art, Design & Media
$ Deerbln Studio

114.01 Down With Design
• Gareth Hardy
◊ Design
$ Right Amount Of Weird

114.02 André Beato
◊ Food & Beverage, Restaurant
$ L´Ours Cocktail Bar

114.03 Backyard 10
◊ Charity
$ Buddybear

115.01 Fuzzco
◊ Food & Beverage
$ Bay Street Biergarten

115.02 Signers
• Pierre Enorm Exner

115.03 Hype Type Studio
• Paul Hutchison, Mark Bloom
◊ Technology
$ U Bear

115.04 Tropenelektronik
◊ Corporate & Business
$ Tüv Rheinland

116.01 Das Buro
◊ Event & Style
$ Edel Amsterdam

116.02 Roy Smith
◊ Design
$ Grizedale Lodge

117.01 Branded | studio for visual communication
◊ Corporate Design
$ Leder Wimmer

118.01 Partly Sunny
◊ Hospitality
$ Rooster

118.02 Salon91
◊ Fashion Store
$ Adler Altona – Herrenboutique

118.03 Indyvisuals
◊ Food, Restaurant
$ Rico's Rottisserie

118.04 Maximilian Baud
◊ Corporate & Business
$ Hotel Schweigerhof

119.01 Chad Michael
◊ Business, Beauty Salon
$ Two Foxes Salon

119.02 indyvisuals
◊ Music, Merchandise
$ Buggsy

119.03 Julian Hrankov
◊ Design
$ Bokk

119.04 The National Grid
◊ Hospitality, Retail
$ Cabassi & Co

120.01 Thonik
◊ Cultural
$ De Appel arts centre

121.01 Thonik
◊ Cultural
$ De Appel arts centre

122.01 Swear Words
◊ Food & Beverage,
$ Minami

122.02 Mondbewohner
◊ Coperate & Cultural
$ Mondbewohner / Wien

122.03 Face
◊ Music
$ Motion Music

122.04 Non-Format
◊ Cultural
$ Ny Musikk

123.01 Swear Words
◊ Food & Beverage
$ Ocean Made Seafood

123.02 Noeeko – Design Studio
◊ Fashion
$ Sailor Clothes

123.03 Andrea Münch
◊ Fashion & Lifestyle
$ The New New, Curated Secondhand

123.04 Cerotreees
• Benkee Chang
◊ Business
$ Waves Surf Shop

123.05 Bleed
• Astrid Feldner
◊ Corporate & Business

124.01 Gravit Art
• Oğuzhan Öçalan
◊ Food

124.02 Werklig
◊ Food & Beverage
$ Helsinki Food Company

124.03 Fontan 2
◊ Food & Beverage
$ Fontan 2

124.04 Tabas
• Cedric Mlo
◊ Ecology
$ Aer

125.01 Rickey Lindberg
◊ Cultural
$ Klap Film

125.02 David Büsser
◊ Corporate & Business, Healthcare
$ Kleintierpraxis M. Rusch

125.03 Zumquadrat – Visuelle Kommunikation
◊ Corporate & Business, Trading
$ Bergische Waren | Gut. Besser. Bergisch

125.04 Unit
◊ Design
$ Pamela Holden

126.01 David Büsser
• David Büsser, Patrik Ferrarelli
◊ Corporate & Business, Healthcare
$ Annette Hamburger

126.02 Eps51 Graphic Design Studio
◊ Corporate
$ Lo Voi — Coiffeur

127.01 Mr Walczuk
◊ Fashion & Lifestyle
$ Pussy Project

127.02 Fons Hickmann m23
◊ Cultural
$ V-Day Berlin 2011

127.03 Tomato Kosir
◊ Cultural Institution
$ Zdravko Duša, Myra Locatelli

128.01 Aro | Christian Schupp
◊ Design
$ Snnc

128.02 Sasha Prood
◊ Food & Beverage
$ Jörgensen & Jörgensen & Undersakers Charkuteriefabrik

128.03 Conspiracy Studio
◊ Fashion
$ Best Kiteboards

128.04 La Tortillería
• Rodrigo Véjar
◊ Restaurant, Food & Beverage
$ Grupo Kampai

129.01 Sunday Vision
◊ Music
$ King Records co., ltd.

129.02 Taeko Isu | Nnnny
◊ Fashion
$ Parco

129.03 Mash
◊ Food & Beverage
$ Cranky Fins Holidae Inn

129.04 Büro Destruct

130.01 Hovercraft Studio
◊ Food, Restaurant
$ Riffle Nw

131.01 The National Grid
◊ Food & Beverage
$ Rocketboy Pizza

131.02 Jeremy Pruitt | Thinkmule
◊ Vintage
$ Thinkmule

131.03 Kanardo
◊ Fashion
$ Sen No Sen

131.04 Kanardo
◊ Fashion
$ Anachronic Clothing

132.01 Franck Juncker | fjopus7
◊ Food & Beverage
$ O Chevreuil Taverne Américaine

132.02 Olivier Charland
◊ Bar, Restaurant
$ Le Nord-Ouest Café

132.03 Swear Words
◊ Food & Beverage
$ The Good Fish

132.04 R2 Design
• Lizá Ramalho, Artur Rebelo
◊ Visual Identity
$ La Paz

133.01 Patrick Molnar
◊ Food & Business

134.01 The National Grid
◊ Food & Beverage
$ Hotel Steyne

134.02 Jeremy Pruitt | Thinkmule
◊ Farming
$ Sailor's Rest Farm

134.03 Pierpaolo Scarpato
◊ Moda
$ Jpierre & Jtod

134.04 Inventaire
◊ Cultural Platform
$ Dzodzet Island

135.01 Ryan Feerer
◊ Media, Technology & Mobile
$ Tiller

135.02 Acre
◊ Maritime
$ Scotia Marine

135.03 Dennis Herzog
◊ Fashion & Lifestyle
$ Trim Collective

135.04 De Jongens Ronner
◊ Food & Beverage
$ Voorwaarts Voorwaarts

136.01 Funnel: Eric Kass
◊ Food & Beverage
$ Lyon Distilling Co.

136.02 Ryan Feerer
◊ Architecture & Interior Design
$ Tom House

136.03 Chad Michael
◊ Chad Michael & Tractorbeam Design
$ Corporate
$ Harvey Ventures

136.04 Vértice Comunicación
• Roberto de Leon, Miriam Ramos
◊ Food & Beverage
$ Casa de Piedra

137.01 Rubén B
◊ Corporate & Business
$ Trust Iberian Lifestyle Especialist

137.02 Jono Garrett

137.03 Jochen Kuckuck
◊ Fashion & Lifestyle
$ Frontlineshop.com

• Designer name, if not identical with studio name   ◊ Category $ Client   © Credits

Work Index   389

137.04 Chad Michael
◊ Business, Alcohol, Whiskey
$ Migrant Whiskey

138.01 Akinori Oishi
◊ Design
$ Animateka
◊ Cultural Institution
$ Origami
◊ Book Title, Design
$ Paperpack

138.02 44flavours
◊ Fashion & Event
$ Party Arty

138.03 Hula + Hula Design
• Cha!
◊ Media, Technology
$ Line

139.01 Jan Moucha / Work-N-Roll
◊ Food & Beverage
$ Mexican Cuisine Restaurant Chain Rancheros

139.02 Maniackers Design | Masayuki Sato
◊ Art & Event
$ Arts Maebashi

139.03 44flavours
◊ Music
$ Shamon Cassette

139.04 Studio Moross
◊ Music
$ Rabble Records

139.05 Cindy T. Mai
◊ Food & Beverage

140.01 Eduardo Vidales
◊ Corporate
$ Top Sandals

140.02 Masa
◊ Fashion & Sports
$ Nike

141.01 Hort
◊ Corporate & Business
$ Cream Colored Ponies

142.01 Struggle inc.
◊ Fashion
$ Quiet Life

142.02 Sellout Industries
• Sebastian Dumjahn
◊ Fashion
$ Adidas Originals

142.03 Jochen Kuckuck
◊ Sports & Lifestyle
$ 2er Skateboarding e.V.

143.01 Nicholaus Jamieson
◊ Fashion
$ Brixton

143.02 Albert Naasner
◊ Fashion
$ Masomaso

143.03 Struggle inc.
◊ Music
$ Bellows Hong Kong

144.01 44flavours
◊ Fashion
$ Oh No Berlin

144.02 Akinori Oishi
◊ Design Exhibition
$ Icc

144.03 George Popov
◊ Record Label
$ Rough Trade

145.01 Chragokyberneticks
◊ Music
$ Son d'été

145.02 Di-Da
• Gotzon Garaizabal
◊ Cultural Institution
$ San Telmo Museoa

145.03 44flavours
◊ Fashion
$ Oh No Berlin

146.01 Noeeko – Design Studio
◊ Food
$ Hot Dog Love

146.02 Noeeko – Design Studio
◊ Food & Beverage
$ Wow Burger Beer

146.03 HappyMess Studio
• Mothi Limbu
◊ Fashion & Kids
$ Underten

147.01 Bergfest
◊ Art
$ Bike Corner

147.02 IS Creative Studio
◊ Music, Cinema
$ Creacción

147.03 Trademark?
◊ Fashion & Lifestyle
$ Money Clothing

150.01 Jon Contino
◊ Non-Profit
$ Evolve
◊ Fashion
$ Whiskey Grade
◊ Food & Beverage
$ Home of the Brave
◊ Vintage
$ Past Lives

151.01 Jon Contino
◊ Sporting Goods
$ Leather Head
◊ Entertainment, Video Games
$ Campo Santo
◊ Product
$ Jon Contino x Word Notebooks
◊ Fashion
$ CXXVI Clothing Co.

152.01 Tyrsa
• Alexis Taieb
◊ Design, Print
$ 99Prints
◊ Sport event
$ La Roue Libre
◊ Izakaya, Food
$ Emon

152.02 Toshikazu Nozaka
◊ Traditional Festival
$ Manazuru-city, music festival association

153.01 Cless
◊ Design & Art
$ El País Newspaper

153.02 designJune
• Julien Crouigneau
◊ Logotype
$ French cowboy

153.03 Sammy Stein
◊ Art
$ Auto Publication

154.01 Sellout Industries
• Sebastian Dumjahn
◊ Fashion
$ Adidas Originals

154.02 Dr. Morbito
• Eric Morales "Odiseo"
◊ Food & Beverage
$ Saydum
◊ Design
$ Tixinda

155.01 Cindy T. Mai
◊ Cultural Institution

155.02 Modo
• Alexander Wright
◊ Music
$ La Maldita Infamia

156.01 Finsta
◊ Media
$ Recmode animation studio

156.02 Cutts Creative
• Hannah Cutts
◊ Fitness
$ Fit Hit

156.03 Braca Burazeri
• Braća Burazeri
◊ Fashion & Lifestyle
$ Dechkotzar Clothing Company

156.04 Laundry
◊ Corporate & Business
$ Flavor

156.05 designJune
• Julien Crouigneau
◊ Logotype
$ French Cowboy

157.01 Förm
◊ Art
$ Slow Slam, Farid Feuerbach

157.02 Alfredo Conrique
◊ Lifestyle
$ Samedi Samedi

157.03 Aldo Lugo
◊ Music
$ Navaja

157.04 Jacques et Brigitte
◊ Fashion & Lifestyle
$ Jacques et Julien haute printûre

157.05 Jeremy Pruitt | Thinkmule
◊ Vintage
$ Thinkmule

158.01 Albert Naasner
◊ Music
$ Wolf Müller

158.02 Hula + Hula Design
• Aldo Lugo
◊ Fashion & Lifestyle
$ Gurú Gallery Shop

158.03 Gonzalo Rodriguez Gaspar
◊ Art
$ Personal Proyect

158.04 Vier5
◊ Art
$ Cac Brétigny

159.01 Anna Magnussen
◊ Lifestyle
$ Monsterklubben

159.02 ['ændi:] Andrea Romano
◊ Corporate & Business, Sport
$ Adil Chihi football player – 1.FC Köln

159.03 Shinpei Onishi
◊ Fashion
$ Wise Middle

160.01 Cabina
◊ Fashion, Shoes, Kids
$ María Urquizu

160.02 Csaba Bernáth
◊ Music & Culture
$ Urban Artforms Hungary

160.03 Anarchy Alchemy
◊ Dirk König
$ Universal Music UK

160.04 Paul Coors
◊ Music
$ Platter Party Records

161.01 Denham
◊ Ali Kirby
◊ Fashion & Lifestyle
$ Denham

162.01 El Solitario
• El Solitario & Maxwell Paternoster
◊ Hard Goods & Special Motorcycles

163.01 El Solitario
• El Solitario & Menze Kwint
◊ Hard Goods & Special Motorcycles

164.01 Chragokyberneticks
◊ Fashion & Lifestyle
$ Yvonne Francesco

164.02 Alessandridesign
$ Gruber Röschitz

165.01 Typejockeys
◊ Food & Beverage
$ Thomas A. Beck

165.02 DesignJune
• Julien Crouigneau
◊ Logotype
$ French cowboy

165.03 Andreas Klammt | 53,5
◊ Corporate & Buisiness
$ Schneider Outdoor Visions

165.04 Teacake Design
• Graham Sykes, Robert Walmsley
◊ Fashion, Tailoring
$ Charles Campbell Bespoke

166.01 Alessandridesign
$ Mazo

166.02 Noeeko – Design Studio
◊ Fashion
$ Insert Brain

166.03 Jeremy Pruitt | Thinkmule
◊ Music
$ Byre Band

167.01 Berger & Föhr
◊ Food & Beverage
$ Jack Rabbit Hill Farm

167.02 Omochi
◊ Fashion & Lifestyle
$ Store Usu

167.03 Max-o-matic
◊ Music
$ Rudo Valdez

167.04 Jonathan Calugi
◊ Music
$ Feline Funk

168.01 Live To Make
◊ Leather Goods and Products
$ Uppercut Deluxe

168.02 Tim Boelaars
◊ Cosmetics
$ Chief's Skincare

168.03 Tim Bjørn
◊ Art
$ Personal

168.04 Triboro Design
◊ Corporate & Business
$ Schmidt Brothers Cutlery

169.01 Jonathan Calugi
◊ Music
$ Hellomynameisrae

170.01 Face
◊ Music
$ Hardpop

170.02 Vonsung
◊ Art consultant
$ Geraldine Cosnuau

170.03 Friedrich Santana Lamego
◊ Art & Design
$ Personnal Project

170.04 Tridente Brand Firm
• Rodo Ramirez
◊ Construction and Technology Industry
$ Ing. Madla

171.01 Tobias Munk
◊ Design
$ Lynild
◊ Corporate & Business
$ Mads Krabbe

171.02 Mehdi Saeedi
171.03 Sawdust
◊ Media, Games, Technology, Design, Art
$ Marshmallow Laser Feast

171.04 Rob Angermuller
◊ Technology
$ Pantheon

171.05 Tim Boelaars
$ Personal use

172.01 Milosz Klimek
◊ Lifestyle, reaction against hunting
$ Forest Life

172.02 Live To Make
◊ Music
$ Joe Causey

173.01 310k
◊ Music
$ Basserk Records, Bronstibock

173.02 Stefano Bracci
◊ Music
$ Mark Bear producer

173.03 Mañana Communication
◊ Design
$ Leona Bolay

173.04 Atelier Dessert
◊ Cultural Institution
$ Kauz

174.01 Heroes Design – Piotr Buczkowski
◊ Media
$ Aggressive.tv

174.02 Brandmor
• Mako Lehel Mor
◊ Food & Beverages
$ Hipermarket Romania

175.01 Zweizehn
• Sven Herkt, Oleg Svidler
◊ Art
$ Self-Intitiated

175.02 100und1
• Lukas Fliszar
◊ Art Exhibition
$ Making Of

176.01 Bureau Mirko Borsche
◊ Cultural Institution
$ Bayerisches Staatsballett

176.02 Bureau Mario Lombardo
• Mario Lombardo
◊ Art & Culture
$ Logo for a two-part exhibition at the Bielefelder Kunstverein

176.03 Heroes Design – Piotr Buczkowski
• Piotr Buczkowski
◊ Art
$ Room Service

176.04 Minigram Studio für Markendesign
◊ Corporate Business
$ Stofanel Investment

177.01 Julianna Goodman / Design + Art Direction (J G / D + A D)
◊ Media, Games, & Technology
$ Super Circle

177.02 Rubén B
◊ Corporate & Business
$ Trust Iberian Lifestyle Especialist

177.03 Canefantasma Studio
◊ Cultural Institution
$ Comune di Genova

177.04 Kissmiklos
◊ Beverage
$ Pastror Winery

178.01 Kissmiklos
◊ Design
$ Soeur PR

178.02 Laundry
◊ Corporate & Business
$ Flavor

178.03 Andreas Neophytou
◊ Fashion & Lifestyle,Culture
$ Hole & Corner magazine

178.04 Deanne Cheuk
◊ Fashion & Lifestyle
$ Sue Stemp

178.05 Kissmiklos
◊ Lifestyle
$ Gabriell & Jean wedding
◊ Food
$ Kiobis

179.01 Kissmiklos
◊ Corporate & Business
$ Bettina Baji; Visual Playground
◊ Fashion
$ Salon1

180.01 Cabina
◊ Spa
$ Four Seasons Hotel Buenos Aires

180.02 Desres Design Group
• Michaela Kessler
◊ Art & Interior
$ Sounds of Silence

180.03 Kissmiklos
◊ Corporate & Business
$ Hungarian British Chamber of Commerce in the United Kingdom

181.01 Vonsung
◊ PR company
$ Communique PR

181.02 Minigram Studio für Markendesign
◊ Corporate & Business
$ Lüthen & Co. Immobilien

181.03 Ccabina
◊ Bar
$ Four Seasons Hotel Buenos Aires

182.01 Passport
◊ Food & Beverage

183.01 Sociodesign
◊ Design
$ Design Business Association

183.02 Family
◊ Corporate
$ Soeur PR

183.03 Homework
◊ Fashion
$ Modezonen

184.01 Manifiesto Futura
◊ Food & Beverage
$ Extravirgen

184.02 Longton
◊ Design
$ Kuca

184.03 Kissmiklos
◊ Fashion
$ Venkavision Blog

184.04 Wanja Ledowski
• Wanja Ledowski, Haruko Sumi
◊ Fashion
$ Edwarda

184.05 Lundgren+Lindqvist
◊ Fashion & Lifestyle
$ Ever rêve

184.06 Maximilian Baud
◊ Corporate & Business
$ Zerzer ceramics

184.07 Unfolded
◊ Architecture
$ Eth Wohnforum – Eth Case

185.01 Manifiesto Futura
◊ Food & Beverage
$ Caguamería

185.02 Fivethousand Fingers
◊ Beverage
$ Dageraad Brewing

185.03 Anagrama
$ Winecast

185.04 Anti / Anti
◊ Sports
$ Harlem Skyscraper Classic

185.05 Bureau Mirko Borsche
◊ Fashion & Lifestyle
$ Horst Magazine

185.06 Homework
◊ Fashion
$ Modezonen

185.07 Anonimo Studio
• Hector Do Nascimento
◊ Corporate & Business
$ Subcultura

185.08 Josiah Jost
◊ Health & Beauty, Spa
$ Organicare Spa

186.01 Tom Grant
◊ Food & Beverage
$ Kitchen Five44

186.02 Brandmor
• Mako Lehel Mor
◊ Food & Beverages, Restaurant, Shop
$ Grano – Food & Care

186.03 Zeroipocrisia
◊ Corporate & Business
$ Insomnia

186.04 ZeCraft
◊ Magazine, Publishing
$ The Walrus

186.05 Homework
◊ Fashion
$ Modezonen

186.06 Werklig
◊ Corporate & Business
$ Finsta Attorneys

186.07 Deutsche & Japaner
◊ Film Production
$ Versal Studios

186.08 Côme de Bouchony
$ Various clients

187.01 ZeCraft
◊ Newspaper & Media
$ The Independent Magazine

187.02 Filmgraphik
◊ Film Title
$ Beauty killed the beast

187.03 Bureau Mirko Borsche
◊ Fashion & Lifestyle
$ The Germans Magazine

187.04 Studio Output
◊ Food & Beverage
$ Macaulay Sinclair

187.05 Antonio Ladrillo
◊ Fashion
$ Billie Sunday

187.06 Swear Words
◊ Corporate & Business
$ Storify

188.01 Homework
◊ Fashion
$ Modezonen

188.02 Face
◊ Food & Beverage
$ Costaoeste

188.03 Espluga+Associates
◊ Food & Beverage
$ Europastry

188.04 Erretres.
◊ Cultural, Branding & Editoial
$ Manuscritics

188.05 Pedro Paulino
◊ Design
$ P/p Studio

• Designer name, if not identical with studio name   ◊ Category $ Client   © Credits

188.06 Bureau Mario Lombardo
◊ Fashion, Art & Culture
$ Logo for Sleek magazine
188.07 Salon91
• Stefan Schröter
◊ Magazine
$ Panthalassa
188.08 Espluga+Associates
◊ Food & Beverage
$ Europastry
189.01 Kissmiklos
◊ Lifestyle
$ The Limited Night
189.02 Alex Trochut
◊ Design, Logo, Label
189.03 Sanscolor
• Joakim Jansson
◊ Desgin
$ Blckmrkt
189.04 ZeCraft
◊ Publishing, Newspaper
$ Le Monde
189.05 Gravit Art
• Oğuzhan Öçalan, Gravitart Design Studio
◊ Lettering & Blog
$ Mesnetsiz Blog
189.05 Genauso.und.anders
◊ Art
$ Buynachten

192.01 Sanscolor
• Joakim Jansson, Bapt ste Ringot
◊ Fashion & Lifestyle
$ Andreas Kleiberg

194.01 Por Amor al Arte
• Iñaki Frías
◊ Health
$ Farmacia Riba
194.02 Onlab
◊ Architecture
$ Wiegelmann-Krammer
194.03 Zumquadrat – Visuelle Kommunikation
◊ Printing press & plant
$ Druckerei Ringeisen
194.04 Ross Gunter
◊ Corporate & Business
$ Kingston House
194.05 Kissmiklos
◊ Fashion
$ Kaldy & Cango

195.01 Cabina
◊ Bar
$ Philippe Sarda
195.02 Aro | Christian Schupp
◊ Music
$ Kid Mac

195.03 Codefrisko
◊ Fashion
$ Louise Leconte
195.04 Pony Design Club
◊ Lifestyle & Sports
$ Rotterdam Pooligans skateboard contest

196.01 Bureau Mario Lombardo
◊ Music & Culture
$ Logo for the music label Film
196.02 Tom Hingston Studio
◊ Jewellery
$ Mappin & Webb
196.03 Denis März
◊ Fashion, Sport, & Bicycle
$ Ion Bike / 3deluxe
196.04 ['ændi:] Andrea Romano
◊ Corporate & Business
$ Oppermann und Weber

197.01 Rüdiger Götz
◊ Fashion
$ Frank Kuhlmann, Marcus Schenkenberg
197.02 R2 Design
• Lizá Ramalho, Artur Rebelo
◊ Visual Identity
197.03 Full Color Canvas
• Jarrod Bryan
◊ Design
$ Toa Distribution
197.04 Wanja Ledowski
◊ Music
$ Dvj

198.01 Tyrsa
• Alexis Taieb
◊ Jewellery
$ Yann-Gael Cobigo
198.02 André Beato
◊ Corporate, Business, Design
$ Personal
198.03 Denis März
◊ Fashion & Sport
$ North Kiteboarding / 3deluxe
198.04 Anagrama
◊ Umutu
198.05 Dennis Herzog
◊ Sport
$ North Kiteboards

199.01 Bureau Lukas Haider
◊ Music & Art
$ Forever In Decay
199.02 Magpie Studio
◊ Television channel
$ 4Seven
199.03 Alex Trochut
◊ Cultural Institution
$ Simple Tipogràfica

199.04 Jon Contino
◊ Food & Beverage
$ Home of the Brave
199.05 indyvisuals
◊ Music
$ Business In Music

200.01 Alex Trochut
200.02 Tyrsa
• Alexis Taieb
◊ Jewellery
$ Samuel Huguenin
200.03 Tyrsa
• Alexis Taieb
◊ Restaurant
$ Aux Deux Cygnes
200.04 Kissmiklos
◊ Fashion
$ Mulika Harnett

201.01 Andrei Robu
◊ Restaurant & Food
$ Red Angus
201.02 Moker
◊ Food & Beverage
$ Jumbo / Od
201.03 Brendan Prince
◊ Design Company
$ Thought Train Creative Group
◊ Food & Beverage
$ SaltHouse Cocktails

202.01 Fons Hickmann m23
◊ Cultural
$ Sony Classical Music
202.02 Glenn Garriock
◊ Food & Beverage
$ Pastatore
202.03 Identity
◊ Food
$ Kalev Chocolate Factory

203.01 Linnea Blixt
◊ Housing tightly compound
$ Brf Gröna gatan 27 – 39
203.02 The National Grid
◊ Food & Beverage
$ Four Frogs Crêperie
203.03 Chad Michael
◊ Business & Beauty Salon
$ The Beauty Kitchen
203.04 Stier Royal
• Christoph Söhne
◊ Corporate & Business, Gastronomy
$ Gastronooom / The Bronx Bar

204.01 Anna-OM-line
◊ Fashion & Lifestyle
$ By.Anna OMline
204.02 Teacake Design
• Graham Sykes / Robert Walmsley
◊ Fashion, Beauty, Retail
$ Tovani Hair
204.03 Acme Industries
◊ Paramon Dițu
◊ Fashion
$ Sophia de Romania
204.04 Live To Make
◊ Film
$ Marfa Peach Co.

205.01 Stitch Design Co.
◊ Hospitality
$ Anne Bowen
205.02 Funnel: Eric Kass
◊ Food & Beverage
$ Velvet Bee Winery
205.03 Mr. Brown – creative boutique
• Artur Augustyniak
◊ Lifestyle & Wedding reception
$ self
205.04 Cutts Creative
• Hannah Cutts
◊ Food & Beverages
$ Girraween wineries

206.01 Stitch Design Co.
◊ Cultural Institution
$ Adam Fetsch
206.02 Csaba Bernáth
◊ Food & Beverage
$ MJ's Treatery
206.03 Maniackers Design | Masayuki Sato
◊ Art & Exhibition
$ Takasaki Museum of Art
206.04 Josiah Jost
◊ Cinema
$ Leclerc Brothers

207.01 Alessandridesign
$ Groszer Wein
207.02 La Tortillería
• La Tortillería
◊ Food
$ Sweet Boutique
207.03 Olsson Barbieri
◊ Beverage & Wine.
$ Symposium Wines As
208.01 Hovard Design
◊ Fashion & Lifestyle, Homegoods & Interior Design
$ Creel and Gow
208.02 Conspiracy Studio
◊ Fashion
$ Hydroponic

208.03 Aro | Christian Schupp
◊ Corporate & Business
$ Vom See
208.04 Kissmiklos
◊ Lifestyle
$ Körben

209.01 Gooqx
◊ Food & Breverge
$ What´s Beef?!
209.02 Bo Lundberg Illustration Ab
◊ Corporate & Business
$ Klockargården
209.03 Base
◊ Fashion
$ Delvaux
209.04 Estudio Soma
◊ Cultural, Television
$ Canal Encuentro

210.01 Olsson Barbieri
◊ Beverage & Wine
$ Vinordia Aa
◊ Beverage & Wine
$ Best Cellars

211.01 Chad Michael
◊ Business, Alcohol, Whiskey
$ Migrant Whiskey
211.02 Hovard Design
◊ Hovard Design
◊ Fashion & Lifestyle, Apothecaries
$ C.O. Bigelow
211.03 Fuzzco
◊ Food & Beverage
$ Thirteenth Colony Distilleries
211.04 Mm75 Design
• Michael Lüthi
◊ Fashion & Lifestyle, Corporate & Business
$ Zee City Syndicate / Mm75 Design

212.01 PolkaGrafik
◊ Food & Beverage
$ Personal
212.02 Graphinya
◊ Lifestyle
$ Floral salon
212.03 Escobas
◊ Food
$ Corporativo Tian de México
212.04 Studio Ah-ha
◊ Fashion & Lifestyle
$ Studio Ah-ha

213.01 **Rickey Lindberg**
◊ Corporate & Business
$ Lejernes Malerfirma

213.02 **Yotam Bezalel Studio**
◊ Corporate Identity
$ Yaffo winery

213.03 **Daniel Blik**
◊ Fashion
$ Látomás

213.04 **Lange & Lange**
◊ CI for Burger Bar

214.01 **Stitch Design Co.**
◊ Fashion & Lifestyle
◊ Food & Beverage
$ Rich Carley and Scott Shore

214.02 **De Jongens Ronner**
◊ Food & Baverge
$ Oestergenootschap

214.03 **Roxane Lagache**
◊ Production, Documentary
$ Alban Teurlai, Thierry Demaizière

215.01 **Irving & Co**
◊ Food & Beverage
$ Rummo Spa

215.02 **Matt Vergotis**
• Matt Vergotis
◊ Food & Beverage
$ Anchorage Restaurant

215.03 **Teacake Design**
• Graham Sykes, Robert Walmsley
◊ Food & Retail
$ Hudson's Ice Cream

215.04 **Dadada Studio**
◊ Fashion & Lifestyle
$ Wool house – local business working with woolen production

216.01 **Roberto Funke**
• Roberto Funke, Julia Hellmann
◊ Corporate & Business
$ Zimmerei Walther Pensold

216.02 **Aro | Christian Schupp**
◊ Corporate & Business
$ Tempus Fugit

216.03 **Verena Michelitsch**
◊ Jewelry Design, Fashion & Lifestyle
$ Bing Bang Jewelry

216.04 **Studio Ah-ha**
◊ Corporate & Business
$ The Handy Man

216.05 **Drach P. Claude**
◊ Hospitality
$ La Hache

217.01 **Studio Ah-ha**
• Studio Ah-ha for Sam Baron & Co
◊ Bed and Breakfast
$ O Val

217.02 **Tomato**
• Dylan Kendle
◊ Fashion & Lifestyle
$ Blanche Dlys Designs

218.01 **Edhv**
◊ Cultural Institution
$ Chv Noordkade

218.02 **Christine Vallaure**
◊ Fashion
$ Achtland

219.01 **Zek**
◊ Shop, Design, Art, Architecture, Products, & Services
$ Rompom

220.01 **Fulguro | Yves Fidalgo & Cédric Decroux**
◊ Achitecture
$ L-Architectes

220.02 **Tomato Kosir**
◊ Art
$ Borut Peterlin

221.01 **Pony Design Club**
◊ Food & Beverages
$ Stielman Coffee Roasters

221.02 **Hort**
◊ Magazine
$ Plot

222.01 **Côme de Bouchony**
$ Various clients

222.02 **HappyMess Studio**
• Mothi Limbu
◊ Fashion
$ Kulte

222.03 **Lldesign**
◊ Fashion
$ Personal work

223.01 **Hort**
◊ Cultural Institution
$ Stiftung Bauhaus Dessau

224.01 **Lundgren+Lindqvist**
◊ Cultural Institution
$ The Photographic Archive

224.02 **Núriavila**
◊ Restaurant & Take away
$ L'encant

224.03 **Thonik**
◊ Cultural Institution & Art
$ Sonsbeek International

225.01 **Albert Naasner**
◊ Art & Books
$ Tfgc Publishing

225.02 **Open Studio**
◊ Cultural Institution
$ Popkultur in Düsseldorf e.V.

228.01 **Base**
◊ Cultural Institution
$ Haus der Kunst

230.01 **TwoPoints.Net**
◊ Food
$ Bacoa

231.01 **TwoPoints.Net**
◊ Food
$ Bacoa

232.01 **Jamie Mitchell**
◊ Architecture
$ Rikkert Paauw, Genevieve Murray

232.02 **Morey Talmor**
◊ Fashion & Lifestyle
$ Oculto

232.03 **Intercity**
◊ Cultural Institution
$ Print-Process

232.04 **Matt Le Gallez**
◊ Design
$ Personal

233.01 **Jamie Mitchell**
◊ Architecture
$ Genevieve Murray

233.02 **Struggle inc.**
◊ Sport
$ Slash Snowboards

233.03 **Stefano Bracci**
◊ Design
$ Gut club

233.04 **Floor 5**
◊ Music
$ Universal Music

234.01 **Dirk König**
◊ Music
$ Universal Music UK

234.02 **Federico Landini**
◊ Fashion & Lifestyle
$ Piero Boano

234.03 **Manifiesto Futura**
◊ Fashion & Lifestyle
$ Pola Foster

234.04 **Piotrek Chuchla**
◊ Art
$ Aleksancer Bruno Gallery

234.05 **Ross Gunter**
◊ Music
$ Aidan Shaw, Toot Sweet

235.01 **Uvmv**
◊ Cultural Institution
$ The Ing Polish Art Foundation

236.01 **Bureau Lukas Haider**
◊ Music & Art
$ Christopher Amott
◊ Music, Art
$ Forever In Decay

236.02 **Loic Sattler**
• Loic Sattler, Lysergid
◊ Dj
$ Jeff Hinchman

236.03 **Red Box Inc.**
• Minji Seo
◊ Fashion & Lifestyle
$ Primaala

236.04 **Nicklas Hultman**
◊ Music
$ House Of Walleberg, Petter Walleberg

236.05 **Vallée Duhamel**
◊ Fashion & Lifestyle
$ Boris & Doris

237.01 **Mind Design**
◊ Restaurant
$ Eclectic

238.01 **Bureau F / Fabienne Feltus**
◊ Corporate & Business
$ Agent Azur-Illustratorenagentur

239.01 **Snask**
◊ Media, Games & Techonolgoy
$ Mobiento

239.02 **George Popov**
◊ Music
$ Work

239.03 **Haltenbanken**
◊ Corporate & Business
$ Audhild Viken

240.01 **Lldesign**
◊ Cultural Institution
$ European Alternatives

240.02 **Faith**
• Paul Sych
◊ Fashion & Lifestyle
$ Fshnunlimited Magazine

240.03 **Stefano Bracci**
◊ Fashion & Lifestyle
$ Isidori Gallery

241.01 **Stahl R**
◊ Corporate & Business
$ Folkdays

241.02 **Manifiesto Futura**
◊ Design
$ Vocero

241.03 **Vier5**
◊ Cultural Institution
$ Jacobs Foundation

241.04 **Trafik**
◊ Cultural Institution
$ Imaginarium

242.01 **Dalston**
◊ Photography
$ Hanna Ukura

242.02 **Dirk König**
◊ Fashion & Lifestyle
$ Antiquerist

242.03 **Akatre**
◊ Cultural & Band music
$ Øliver

242.04 **Non-Format**
◊ Exhibition Identity
$ Shoot Gallery

242.05 **Dirk König**
◊ Music
$ Institute of Harmless Thinking

243.01 **Stefano Bracci**
◊ Fashion & Lifestyle
$ Isidoro Galley

243.02 **Studio Ah-ha**
◊ Corporate & Events
$ Adema

243.03 **100und1**
• Maximilian Huber
◊ Media Artist
$ Nina Mengin

243.04 **John Langdon**
◊ Corporate & Business
$ Perme8

243.05 **Floor 5**
◊ Fashion
$ Dawn Denim

243.06 **Gianni Rossi**
◊ Photography, Video, Fashion
$ Samoo

245.01 **Raum Mannheim**
◊ Corporate & Business
$ Di.natives

246.01 **Nohemi Dicuru**
◊ Fashion
$ Nohemi Dicuru

246.02 **Bureau Hardy Seiler**
• Hardy Seiler
◊ Corporate & Business
$ Freies Theater Hannover

246.03 **Wanja Ledowski**
• Wanja Ledowski, Haruko Sumi
◊ Cultural Institution
$ Médiathèque du Kremlin-Bicêtre

Work Index

• Designer name, if not identical with studio name   ◊ Category $ Client   © Credits

247.01 **Pony Design Club**
◇ Cultural Institution
$ Skvr
247.02 **Carsten Giese | Studio Regular**
◇ Conference
$ Udk Berlin
247.03 **Manifiesto Futura**
◇ Art
$ Cacá Santoro
247.04 **Bleed**
◇ Real estate
$ Norwegian Property

248.01 **Kokoro & Moi**
◇ Cultural Institution
$ The Kennedy Center

249.01 **Büro Uebele**
• Philipp Schäfer, Andreas Uebele
◇ Education
249.02 **Fivethousand Fingers**
◇ Art
$ Black Visual Archive
249.03 **Trademark?**
◇ Art
$ Basement Press
249.04 **Anagrama**
$ Novelty

250.01 **Bureau Malte Metag**
• Malte Metag
◇ Location, Art & Lifestyle
$ Island
250.02 **Richard Baird**
◇ Architecture
$ Barale+Sinibaldi Architetti
250.03 **Raum Mannheim**
◇ Cultural Institution
$ Koenig – Buero fuer Kunst
250.04 **La Tigre**
◇ Design
$ ArcArreda

251.01 **Brogen Averill**
◇ Design & Photography
$ Mara Sommer
251.02 **Making Waves**
◇ Fashion & Lifestyle
$ Bonnier, Stylista
251.03 **Bureau Mirko Borsche**
◇ Cultural Institution
$ Symphonieorchester des Bayerischen Rundfunks
251.04 **Akatre**
◇ Cultural
$ L'Onde Théâtre Centre d'Art

252.01 **Bureau Mirko Borsche**
◇ Cultural Institution
$ Platform München
252.02 **E-Types A/S**
◇ Culture
$ FabLab

253.01 **Richard Baird**
◇ Photography
$ Taryn Grey
253.02 **Jonathan Zawada**
◇ Design
$ Jonathan Zawada
253.03 **Studio Moross**
◇ Music
$ Landshapes, Bella Union
253.04 **Re-public**
• Romeo Vidner
◇ Architecture
$ Alex Poulsen Arkitekter

254.01 **Eps51 Graphic Design Studio**
◇ Corporate
$ M4 Models
254.02 **Lee Goater**
◇ Dance, Arts & Culture
$ Northern School of Contemporary Dance
254.03 **Anti**
◇ Sport, Corporate
$ Birkebeinerrennet

255.01 **Ropp**
• Ropp Schouten
◇ Cultural Initiative, Music
$ Het geluid van Rotterdam
255.02 **Salutpublic**
255.03 **Anti**
◇ Sport & Corporate
$ Birkebeinerrennet

256.01 **Fulguro | Yves Fidalgo & Cédric Decroux**
◇ Cultural Center
$ Datcha
256.02 **Francesc Moret**
◇ Fashion
$ Thinkingmu

257.01 **Ryan Feerer**
◇ Art & Photography
$ Isabelle Selby Photography
257.02 **Stefano Bracci**
◇ Music
$ Ceasars Productions
257.03 **Manifiesto Futura**
◇ Corporate & Business
$ Erosión
257.04 **Kanardo**
◇ Fashion
$ Anachronic Clothing

258.01 **Lidesign**
◇ Cultural Institution
$ Cinemovel Foundation
258.02 **Mondbewohner**
◇ Cultural & Lifestyle
$ Free
258.03 **Mondbewohner**
$ Analog Sonntag/Workshopreihe
258.04 **100und1**
• 100und1, Lukas Fliszar
◇ Short Film
$ Project Homophobia

259.01 **Albert Naasner**
◇ Music
$ Themes For Great Cities Records
259.02 **The National Grid**
◇ Food & Beverage
$ The Char Rotisserie
259.03 **Kelly D. Williams**
◇ Fashion & Lifestyle
$ Proper Burial Brand
259.04 **Anagrama**
$ Prehispência

260.01 **Struggle inc.**
◇ Food & Beverage
$ Yardbird Restaurant Hong Kong
260.02 **The National Grid**
◇ Retail, Fashion
$ Wild Things Gallery
260.03 **A-Side Studio**
◇ Design
$ A-Side Studio
260.04 **Albin Holmqvist**
◇ Film & Art
$ Gustav Johansson/Nokia
260.05 **Nicklas Hultman**
◇ Food & Beverages
$ Santa Maria
260.06 **Quinta-Feira**
◇ Music
$ Digitaldubs

261.01 **Tobias Munk**
◇ Music
$ Clara
261.02 **Quinta-Feira**
◇ Music
$ Dub'Oldin
261.03 **Albert Naasner**
◇ Entertainment & Art
$ Michael Krisch Magic
261.04 **George Popov**
◇ Music
$ Young Hare
261.05 **Kanardo**
◇ Fashion
$ Bask in the Sun

262.01 **Chragokyberneticks**
◇ Music
$ Artlu Bubble and the Dead Animal Gang
262.02 **Studio Moross**
◇ Music
$ Wild life, Method music
262.03 **100und1**
• Maximilian Huber
◇ Open Air Festival
$ Tanz Durch Den Tag
262.04 **Alfredo Conrique**
◇ Music & Lifestyle
$ Pepsi

263.01 **Alfredo Conrique**
◇ Cultural & Music
$ Latin Kustom Festival
263.02 **Alfredo Conrique**
◇ Cultural & Art
$ Mercadorama
263.03 **Via Grafik**
• Leo Volland
◇ Music
$ Self
263.04 **Andrei Robu**
◇ Art
$ Typeverything

264.01 **Mind Design**
◇ Fashion
$ Feral Sphere

265.01 **Mind Design**
◇ Fashion
$ Feral Sphere

268.01 **Kokoro & Moi**
◇ Cultural Institution
$ Pro Arte Foundation

269.01 **Kokoro & Moi**
◇ Cultural Institution
$ Pro Arte Foundation

270.01 **Zweizehn**
• Christian Schreiber
◇ Music
$ BigRig Festival

271.01 **Bravo Company**
◇ Food & Beverages
$ Mexout

272.01 **Rudi de Wet**
◇ Art & Design
$ Siân Darling

273.01 **Hula + Hula Design**
• Aldo Lugo
◇ Music
$ Sony Music

273.02 **Masa**
◇ Music
$ Holger
273.03 **Brand New History?**
$ Lifetime Collective
273.04 **Johan Thuresson**
◇ Design
$ Zebraapa

274.01 **Sweyda**
• Jared Mirabile
◇ Custom lettering, Apparel
$ Nesian Street Clothing
◇ Eyewear, custom lettering, monogram
$ Van Rocca Eyewear
274.02 **Tyrsa**
• Alexis Taïeb
◇ Music
$ F.a.l.d
274.03 **Denis März**
◇ Sports, Design
$ North Kiteboarding

275.01 **Sweyda**
• Jared Mirabile
◇ Custom lettering, Motorcycles, & Dare Devil
$ Evel Knievel
◇ Custom lettering, Music & Dj
$ Jane Bang
275.02 **Andrei Robu**
◇ Art
$ Typeverything
275.03 **Dtm_Inc**
◇ Fashion
$ Fox Productions

276.01 **Super Top Secret**
◇ Food & Beverage
$ Publik Coffee Roasters
◇ Food & Beverage
$ The Garage Bar & Grill
276.02 **Alfredo Conrique**
◇ Art
$ Black Celebration
276.03 **Gitte Thrane**
◇ Cultural Institution
$ KulturMarkt

277.01 **Double Standards**
◇ Cultural Institution
$ Theater der Welt Mannheim

278.01 **Rudi de Wet**
◇ Art & Design
$ Michael Tan aka My Uncle
278.02 **Struggle inc.**
◇ Fashion
$ Quiet Life

278.03 Kelly D. Williams
◊ Art
$ Altamont
278.04 Digitaluv
• Nc Stormgaard
◊ Design
$ Arkitektur Ministeriet

279.01 Irving & Co
◊ Hospitality
$ Giraffe
279.02 Jordy van den Nieuwendijk
◊ Music
$ Fantastic Fantastic
◊ Music
$ Boef en de Gelogeerde Aap
◊ Corporate & Business
$ Hans Konings

280.01 Modo
• Alexander Wright
◊ Design
$ Self
280.02 Simon Seidel
◊ Cultural Institution
$ Amaphiko
280.32 Andreas Neophytou
◊ London Underground
$ Transport for London

281.01 Modo
• Alexander Wright
◊ Music
$ Malangat
◊ Design
$ Modovisual
281.02 Karol Gadzala is YLLV
• Marta Podkowinska
◊ Design
$ Wetransfer.com
281.03 Acme Industries
• Paramon Ditu
◊ Technology
$ Proximuse

282.01 Torrents
◊ Cultural
$ Cap nen sense plat
282.02 Haigh + Martino
• Dylan Haigh
◊ Cultural Institution
$ Children's Museum of New Hampshire
282.03 Escobas
◊ Food
$ Restaurants Toks
282.04 Europa
◊ Architecture & Research studio
$ Dk-Cm Architects

283.01 Büro Destruct
283.02 Heydays
◊ Corporate & Business
$ Intu
283.03 Heroes Design – Piotr Buczkowski
◊ Fashio & Lifestyle
$ Pracownia Kreatywna La La La

284.01 Sasha Prood
• Sasha Prood
◊ Media, Game & Technology
$ Maxim Magazine

285.01 Jon Kennedy
• Marcus Fletcher
◊ Music, Branding
$ Jon Kennedy
285.02 Sasha Prood
◊ Food & Beverage
$ Food & Wine Magazine
285.03 Toshikazu Nozaka
◊ Izakaya, Food
$ Emon
285.04 Jun Kaneko
◊ Music
$ Space orbit
285.05 Bold Stockholm
◊ Corporate & Business
$ Sempre

286.01 Bond Creative Agency Oy
• Jesper Bange, James Zambra, Toni Hurme
◊ Education & Culture
$ University of the Arts Helsinki

288.01 Hopa studio
• Marcin Paściak, Piotr Hołub
◊ Art & Event
$ Ars Thanea

289.01 Tyler Quarles
◊ Sports Lifestyle
$ Capita Snowboarding
289.02 Trapped in Suburbia
◊ Property repurposing
$ Mark van de Broek
289.03 HappyMess Studio
• Mothi Limbu,
◊ Fashion
$ Kulte
289.04 Via Grafik
• André Nossek
◊ Music
$ Presto – Essential Drum'n'Bass
289.05 Kokoro & Moi
◊ Technology
$ AddSearch

289.06 Coup
◊ Dance
$ Leine Roebana

290.01 Trapped in Suburbia
◊ Design
$ Trapped in Suburbia

291.01 Pierre Vanni
◊ Cultural, Music
$ Les Siestes Électroniques
291.02 Jonathan Zawada
◊ Music
$ Mark Pritchard
291.03 Attak
◊ Design
$ Onomatopee
291.04 Kokoro & Moi
◊ Food & Beverage
$ Torikorttelit

292.01 Oblique
◊ Culture & Artist
$ Maxim Frank
292.02 Sabina Keric
• Ready Made
◊ Art
292.03 Commune
◊ Fashion & Lifestyle
$ Kiitos
292.04 Tomato
• Simon Taylor
◊ Music
$ Five Man Army

293.01 Taeko Isu | Nnnny
◊ Life style shop
$ Parco
293.02 Dirk König
• Vera Brych
◊ Corporate & Business, Design
$ Turbo Laser
293.03 Walter Giordano
• Keith Hamworth, Gordon Bleu
◊ Fashion, Art & Gallery, Corporate, Brand Identity, Life, Sport
$ Pro Club
• Proemotional
◊ Fashion, Art, & Gallery, Corporate, Brand Identity
$ Proemotional

294.01 Aro | Christian Schupp
◊ Fashion & Lifestyle
$ Teer clothing
294.02 Federico Landini
◊ Music
$ Me & You

294.04 Anarchy Alchemy
• Dirk König
◊ Music
$ Universal Music UK
295.01 Non-Format
◊ Exhibition Identity
$ Shoot Gallery
295.02 Bureau Mirko Borsche
◊ Cultural Institution
$ Pinakothek der Moderne
295.03 Non-Format
◊ Exhibition Identity
$ Shoot Gallery

296.01 ZeCraft
◊ Fashion
$ Louis Vuitton Malletier
296.02 Oat Creative Design Studio
• Jennifer Lucey-Brzoza
◊ Food & Beverage
$ Saloon
296.03 Stitch Design Co.
◊ Fashion & Lifestyle
$ Rebekka Seale
296.04 Bureau Mario Lombardo
◊ Fashion & Culture
$ KaDeWe

297.01 Fivethousand Fingers
◊ Fashion
$ Dodge and Burn
297.02 Alessandridesign
◊ Cinema
$ Le Grand Bal
297.03 Tyrsa
• Alexis Taïeb
◊ Cinema
$ Moonshaker
297.04 Werklig
◊ Food & Beverage
$ Navy Jerry's Bar & Restaurant

298.01 Anagrama
$ Galo Kitchen
298.02 Fairchildesign
◊ Food & Beverage
$ Deep River Snacks
298.03 Alejandro Paul
◊ Fashion Brand
$ Alias Clothing
298.04 Sergey Shapiro
◊ Design
$ They Integrated Inc.
298.05 Konstantinos Gargaletsos
◊ Corporate & Business
$ Southerly
298.06 Erretres.
• Strategy, Branding, Packaging & Communication
$ Negocios Raros

299.01 Anagrama
$ Los Tacos Azulos
299.02 Haigh + Martino
• Brett Stenson, Dylan Haigh
◊ Food & Beverage
$ Vida Cantina
299.03 Inkgraphix
◊ Music
$ Personal project
299.04 Werklig
◊ Corporate & Business
$ Erimover
299.05 Oat Creative Design Studio
• Jennifer Lucey-Brzoza
◊ Food & Beverage
$ Fletcher's
299.06 Inkgraphix
◊ Games
$ Orcbite

300.01 Dirk König
• Vera Brych
◊ Design, Fashion & Lifestyle
$ Turbo Laser
300.02 Gonzalo Rodriguez Gaspar
◊ Fashion & Lifestyle
$ Number Ten
300.03 Brendan Prince
◊ Athletic team
$ Attitude, Pink Ribbon Breast Cancer Walk
300.04 Andrei Robu
◊ Art
$ Typeverything
300.05 Ortografika
◊ Fashion & Lifestyle
$ Mimitu

301.01 Codefrisko
◊ Bar
$ Sporting
301.02 Sergey Shapiro
◊ Media, Games, Entertainment & Advertisement
$ Harrington & Sons Inc.
301.03 Peter Steffen
◊ Fashion & Lifestyle
$ Fatum surfboard, Fenchurch, Cell, Fallen Hero.
301.04 Aro | Christian Schupp
◊ Design
$ We Cheese You

Work Index 395

• Designer name, if not identical with studio name   ◊ Category $ Client   © Credits

302.01 Daniel Blik
◊ Food & Beverage
$ RothBeer Brewery
302.02 Maria Lyng
◊ Corporate & Business
$ Salling
302.03 Inkgraphix
◊ Music
$ Mack Beats
302.04 Pony Design Club
◊ Film, Stop Motion Animation
$ Trimtab Pictures
302.05 Noeeko – Design Studio
◊ Fashion
◊ Crogo
◊ Art
$ Soho

303.01 Atelier Dessert
◊ Fashion & Lifestyle
$ Urban Plants
303.02 Andrei Robu
◊ Art
$ Typeverything
303.03 Aro | Christian Schupp
◊ Design
$ Aro
303.04 La Tortillería
◊ Fashion
$ Lemon Chic
303.05 Maria Lyng
◊ Design & Lifestyle
$ JC Conda
303.06 Aro | Christian Schupp
◊ Fashion & Lifestyle
$ Young Guerrilla Movement
303.07 Christine Vallaure
◊ Design
$ Christine Vallaure

304.01 Snask
◊ Food & Beverage
$ Debaser

305.01 Andrew Woodhead
◊ Food & Beverage
$ Jackets
305.02 Oat Creative Design Studio
• Jennifer Lucey-Brzoza
◊ Fashion & Lingerie
$ Edge O' Beyond
305.03 Quique Ollervides
◊ Music
$ Arts & Crafts Mexico, Beach House
305.04 Mgmt design
◊ Food & Beverage
$ Elbow Room
305.05 Maria Lyng
◊ Food & Beverage
$ Ba Project

306.01 Sergey Shapiro
◊ Corporate & Business.
$ Deux
◊ Media, Technology & Application
$ Better Labs, Inc.
306.02 Gooqx
◊ Corporate, Business, Fashion & Lifestyle
$ Gooqx
306.03 IS Creative Studio
◊ Food & Beverage
$ Passion Restaurant
306.04 Studio Moross
◊ Music
$ Kid A
◊ Music
$ Monday Records / Tourist
306.05 Calligrapher Mami
◊ Art
$ Monday Art Club

307.01 Toben
◊ Hospitality, Food, & Drink
$ The Reformatory Caffeine Lab
307.02 Noeeko – Design Studio
◊ Food
$ Sleep All Day
307.03 100und1
◊ 100und1, Maximilian Huber
$ Fine Jewellery Reseller
$ By Sergej
307.04 Inkgraphix
◊ Music
$ Warner Music
307.05 La Tortillería
◊ La Tortillería
$ Design
$ Rajeev Shinh

308.01 Bmd Design
• Bmd Design, Bruno Michaud
◊ Fuel Bespoke Motorcycles
$ Fuel Bespoke motorcycles

309.01 Bmd Design
• Bmd Design, Bruno Michaud
◊ Fuel Bespoke Motorcycles Scram, Tracker.
$ Fuel Bespoke motorcycles

310.01 Bmd Design
• Bmd Design, Bruno Michaud
◊ Fashion
$ Yasakin

311.01 Bmd Design
• Bruno Michaud
◊ Fashion
$ This Indian Summer
$ Tank Garage Winery
◊ Branding Campaign
$ Upland Brewing Co.

312.01 Bmd Design
• Bmd Design, Bruno Michaud
$ Upland Brewing Co.

313.01 Bmd Design
• Bruno Michaud
◊ Upland Branding Campaign
◊ Branding Campaign
$ Upland Brewing Co.

314.01 Sergey Shapiro
◊ Music
$ Erick Diaz, Dj
◊ Design & Illustration
$ Mike Chenut
314.02 Tyler Quarles
◊ Corporate
$ Telus
314.03 Manifiesto Futura
◊ Music
$ Rock On Fire

315.01 Tyler Quarles
◊ Literature
$ Lauren Camp
315.02 Ilovedust
◊ Media, Games & Technology
$ Microsoft
315.03 Aldo Lugo
◊ Media
$ Toni François
315.04 21bis
• Frank Dresmé, Stefan van den Heuvel
◊ Sports & Magazine
$ Taste Snowboard Magazine

316.01 Jon Contino
◊ Wine
$ The Hidden Sea

318.01 Anagrama
$ Habibis
318.02 Ali Khorshidpour
◊ Corporate & Business
$ Khojasteh Co.
◊ Cultural Institution
$ Charity Foundation

319.01 Eps51 Graphic Design Studio
◊ Cultural
$ Al Riwaq Art Space Bahrain
319.02 Ali Khorshidpour
◊ Design
$ Imperial Interior Design
◊ Cultural Institution
$ Research Institute of Culture, Art and Communication

320.01 Eyal Baumert
◊ Lifestyle, Organic Cosmetics
$ Arugot Organic Cosmetics

321.01 Eyal Baumert
◊ Food & Beverage
$ Cordovero Brewery

322.01 Yasuwo Miyamura
◊ Music
$ Hiroshi Suzuki
◊ Art
$ Akuma no shirushi

323.01 Foreign Policy Design Group
◊ Cultural Institution
$ Sifang Art Museum, Nanjing, China
323.02 Yasuwo Miyamura
$ Yasuaki & Kao
323.03 Non-Format
◊ Exhibition Identity
$ Tokyo Type Directors Club

324.01 Yasuwo Miyamura
• Yu Miyama
◊ Art
$ Kotubu momoyamajo
324.02 Jaemin Lee
◊ Cultural Institution
$ Junglim Foundation
324.03 Uji Design
◊ Carpenter & Architect
$ Ono-Kosho
324.04 Yasuwo Miyamura
◊ Art
$ Akuma no shirushi

325.01 Yasuwo Miyamura
◊ Media
$ Fusosha
325.02 Calligrapher Mami
◊ Music
$ Shing02
325.03 Yasuwo Miyamura
◊ Design
$ Fujiwalabo
◊ Art
$ Akuma no shirushi

326.01 Verena Michelitsch
◊ Surf, Sports, Movie, Documentary
$ The Old, the Young and the Sea Film Crew
326.02 Rickey Lindberg
◊ Corporate & Business
$ Our Carpenter
326.03 Feed
◊ Members club
$ Club Mont-Royal

326.04 Wanja Ledowski
◊ Food & Beverage
$ Marcovaldo

327.01 Olsson Barbieri
◊ Food
$ Bamsrudlåven

328.01 Stier Royal
• Christoph Söhnel
◊ Food & Beverage
$ Gastronooom, Stier Royal
328.02 Rom Studio
• Rodrigo Maceda
$ Philip Morris
328.03 Rom Studio
• Rodrigo Maceda
◊ Food & Berverage
$ Grupo Modelo / Suma web
328.04 Aro | Christian Schupp
◊ Fashion & Lifestyle
$ Hook Clothing

329.01 Konstantinos Gargaletsos
◊ Music
$ Hoop Music
329.02 ['ændi:] Andrea Romano
◊ Corporate & Business, Food & Beverage
$ 3h's burger & chicken
329.03 Quique Ollervides
◊ Food & Beverage
$ Séptimo
329.04 Milosz Klimek
◊ Fashion & Lifestyle
$ Watch Merchant

330.01 Magpie Studio
• Magpie Studio, Here Design
◊ Food & Beverage
$ London's Brewing Festival
330.02 Ryan Feerer
◊ Design
$ Beer Brothers
◊ Food & Beverage
$ Pappy Slokum

331.01 Ryan Feerer
◊ Food & Beverage
331.02 De Jongens Ronner
◊ Food
$ Maallust

332.01 Anti / Anti
◊ Sports
$ Harlem Skyscraper Classic

332.02 Max-o-matic
◊ Music
$ Miqui Puig, Lav Records

332.03 Alen 'Type08' Pavlovic
• Alen Pavlovic
◊ Fashion & Lifestyle
$ Bike Villains

332.04 Anti / Anti
◊ Sports
$ Harlem Skyscraper Classic
◊ Sports
$ Harlem Skyscraper Classic

333.01 Noeeko – Design Studio
◊ Lifestyle
$ Mr Hovobta

333.02 Ilovedust
◊ Fashion & Lifestyle
$ Mutt Motorcycles

334.01 Patrick Molnar
◊ Fashion
$ Zur Anprobe

334.02 Chris Rubino
◊ Fashion & Corporate Responsibility
$ Gap

334.03 Is Creative Studio
• Is Creative Studio
◊ Food & Beverage
$ Pezca Restaurant

334.04 Kissmiklos
◊ Fashion
$ AnnaAmélie

335.01 Bold Stockholm
◊ Fashion & Lifestyle
$ The Shirt Factory

336.01 Zweizehn
• Sven Herkt, Oleg Svidler
◊ Corporate & Business
$ Institut Praehistorica

337.01 HappyMess Studio
• Mothi Limbu
◊ Fashion
$ True Playa'z Show Room

337.02 Yu Ping Chuang
• Yu Ping Chuang
◊ Lifestyle & Cosmetics
$ Tivoli

337.03 Alessandridesign
$ Wachter-Wiesler

337.04 Mash
◊ Corporate & Business
$ Fireball Printing

338.01 Shinpei Onishi
◊ Food
$ Kuki's Granola Granola

338.02 Swsp Design
• Georg Schatz
◊ Art
$ Sabine Eichbauer

338.03 Anagrama
$ Piper and Sons

338.04 Tarzan + Jane
◊ Design, Art
$ Tina & Patrik

339.01 Meyer Miller Smith
• Carsten Schneider, Lars Eberle
◊ Digital craftsmanship & Design
$ Meyer, Miller, Smith

339.02 Oat Creative Design Studio
• Jennifer Lucey-Brzoza
◊ Fashion & Lingerie
$ Harlow & Fox

339.03 One Design
◊ Wine 339
$ Treasury Wine Estates

340.01 Roxane Lagache
◊ Organic food & Beverage
$ Maud Zilnyk

341.01 Conspiracy Studio
◊ Art
$ Conspiracystudio

341.02 Chad Michael
◊ Business & Photography
$ Mirko Merchiori

341.03 Conspiracy Studio
◊ Art
$ Conspiracystudio

341.04 310k
◊ Music
$ Basserk Records/LeVingtQuatre

341.05 Live To Make
◊ Photography
$ Love, The Nelsons

342.01 Lange & Lange
◊ Ci for American style Restaurant
$ Bydlo i Powidlo

342.02 Jaemin Lee
• Heesun Kim, Jaemin Lee, Hezin Oh, Eunji Lim, Woogyung Geel, Hwayoung Lee, Hyehyun Yi
◊ Fashion & Lifestyle
$ LG Fashion

342.03 Gaetan Billault
◊ Food & Fish and Chips Diner
$ Friendly Fish

343.01 Karolis Kosas
◊ Food
$ Chocolate Naive

343.02 Csaba Bernáth
◊ Hospitality
$ David's Barbershop

343.03 Anagrama
$ Hawaii Cinco Cero

343.04 Andrei Robu
◊ Restaurant
$ Bread & Spices

344.01 Christianconlh
◊ Food & Beverage
$ Serial Griller

344.02 Mash
◊ Food & Beverage
$ Meat & Livestock Australia

345.01 Mikey Burton
◊ Food, Editorial & Design
$ Esquire

346.01 High Tide
• High Tide, Danny Miller
◊ Fashion & Lifestyle
$ Nike

347.01 Funnel: Eric Kass
• Eric Kass
◊ Fashion & Lifestyle, Vintage Antique Store
$ Society of Salvage

347.02 Metastazis.com
◊ Music
$ Behemoth

347.03 Metastazis.com
◊ Music
$ Peste Noire

347.04 Chad Michael
◊ Business, Apparel
$ Striven Clothing

348.01 Tobias Munk
◊ Design
$ Tobias Munk Åkesson

348.02 Ludlow Kingsley
◊ City & Government
$ The City of Santa Monica

348.03 Gonzalo Rodriguez Gaspar
◊ Art & Lifestyle
$ Mad Mind Wear

348.04 Manifiesto Futura
◊ Food & Beverage
$ Perro Malo

349.01 Calango
◊ Music
$ Sono Sanctus

349.02 Kanardo
◊ Fashion
$ Sen No Sen

349.03 Andrei Robu
◊ Restaurant & Food
$ Red Angus

349.04 Chad Michael
◊ Business & Clothing
$ Soho Six Apparel

350.01 Homework
◊ Fashion
$ Modezonen

350.02 Andreas Töpfer
◊ Music
$ Ignaz Schick

350.03 Albert Naasner
◊ Sports
$ Tischtennis Club Germania Fürstenplatz 09

350.04 Olsson Barbieri
◊ Identity for Coffee Bar in Oslo
$ Bang Chau Kaffeforetning

351.01 Bergfest
• Ari Bolk, Jens Uwe Meyer
◊ Fashion & Lifestyle
$ Stiebich & Rieth

351.02 Codefrisko
◊ Hair industry
$ L'Atelier Blanc

351.03 Csaba Bernáth
◊ Art
$ Mahinárium

351.04 Noeeko – Design Studio
◊ Fashion
$ One Half

352.01 Cchristianconlh
◊ Art
$ Lars Moereels

352.02 Live To Make
◊ Music
$ Colony House

352.03 Ineo Designlab
◊ Fashion & Lifestyle
$ Højmark Cycles

353.01 Das.Graphiker
• Ana Camacho at Das.Graphiker
◊ Design

354.01 Mikey Burton
◊ Design, Fasion, & Lifestyle
$ Anthony Baratta

354.02 Rubén B
◊ Corporate & Business
$ Slow Life Hàbitat Social Sostenible

354.03 Andreas Klammt | 53,5
◊ Art
$ Cyan collective

354.04 Büro Glöwing
◊ Food
$ Tofutown

354.05 Via Grafik
• Lars Herzig
◊ Cultural Institution
$ Klima-Bündnis, Climate Alliance, Alianza del Clima

354.06 Raum Mannheim
◊ Music
$ Jankovic & Pender

354.07 Jonathan Calugi
◊ Art
$ Lovers town

354.08 Jamie Mitchell
◊ Architecture
$ Genevieve Murray

354.09 Alen 'Type08' Pavlovic
• Alen Pavlovic
◊ Design
$ Design on Tap

354.10 Gianmarco Magnani
◊ Surf
$ Wave Surfboards

355.01 Rob Angermuller
◊ Fashion & Lifestyle
$ Firelily

355.02 Conspiracy Studio
◊ Corporate
$ Cece Surfboards

355.03 Albin Holmqvist
◊ Hospitality
$ Lawrence Marquez

355.04 Áron Jancsó
◊ Fashion
$ Clear Tha Karma

355.05 Face
◊ Art
$ L'Art de Vivre

355.06 Andreas Klammt | 53,5
◊ Corporate & Buisiness
$ Andreas Klammt

355.07 Family
◊ Lifestyle
$ Miler + Greig

355.08 Bergfest
• Ari Bolk, Jens Uwe Meyer
◊ Food
$ Die Tortenmanufaktur

355.09 Laundry
◊ Corporate & Business
$ Kingsbury

355.10 Cabina
◊ Bar
$ Four Seasons Hotel Buenos Aires

Work Index 397

• Designer name, if not identical with studio name   ◊ Category $ Client   © Credits

356.01 Busybuilding
◊ Food & Beverage
$ Akis Petretzikis

356.02 Bureau Malte Metag
◊ Corporate & Business
$ David Felsmann

356.03 Aro | Christian Schupp
◊ Design
$ Snnc

356.04 Cabina
◊ Hotel & Events
$ Four Seasons Hotel Buenos Aires

356.05 Alter
◊ Lifestyle, Fitness & Sport, Wellbeing
$ One Hot Yoga

356.06 Bianca Dumitrascu
◊ Personal Identity, Corporate & Business
$ Bianca Dumitrascu

356.07 Face
◊ Architecture
$ Adrian Key

356.08 Swsp Design
• Georg Schatz
◊ Food & Beverage
$ Ludwig Schatz

356.09 Jules Césure
• Julien Borean & Cécile Vanhoolandt
◊ Design, Art
$ Jules Césure

356.10 Julianna Goodman / Design + Art Direction (J G / D + A D)
◊ Food & Beverage
$ Trace and Trust

356.11 Andreas Klammt | 53,5
◊ Music
$ Monaco à Go-Go

356.12 Demetrio Mancini
◊ Food & Beverage
$ Officina del Sole

356.13 Brandmor
• Mako Lehel Mor
◊ Design
$ Brandmor

357.01 Deutsche & Japaner
◊ Music
$ Beatgees, Producer & Songwriter

357.02 Anna Magnussen
◊ Art

357.03 Black-Marmalade
◊ Prevention Organization
$ The Love Company Group

357.04 Alen 'Type08' Pavlovic
• Alen Pavlovic
◊ Music
$ Channelside Records

358.01 Longton
• Michael Longton
◊ Design
$ Self

359.01 Longton
• Michael Longton
◊ Food & Beverage
$ Sample Brew

360.01 Bureau Mirko Borsche
◊ Cultural Institution
$ Bayerisches Staatsballett

361.01 Bureau Mirko Borsche
◊ Cultural Institution
$ Bayerische Staatsoper

362.01 Chris Henley
◊ Corporate & Business, Design
$ Good+Brave

362.02 High Tide
• High Tide, Danny Miller
◊ Fashion & Lifestyle
$ Breyburn

362.03 Clusta
◊ Music
$ Rising Music

362.04 BankerWessel
• Jonas Banker, Ida Wessel
◊ Corporate & Business
$ Alessandro Ripellino Arkitekter / Järngrinden

362.05 Calango
$ De Staalkade Zes

362.06 Bureau F / Fabienne Feltus
◊ Corporate & Business
$ Sandra Jedliczka Photographer

362.07 Unit
◊ Design & Art
$ Colours May Vary

362.08 Raum Mannheim
◊ Music, Corporate Design
$ Prisma Music

362.09 Brandmor
• Mako Lehel Mor
◊ Corporate & Business
$ Ana-Maria Iacob Advocate

362.10 Cabina
◊ Music Label
$ Stephan Mathieu

362.11 Brogen Averill
◊ Design
$ McLellan Jacobs

362.12 Áron Jancsó
◊ Fashion
$ Clear Tha Karma

362.13 Calango
◊ Fashion & Styling
$ Alter

362.14 Backyard 10
◊ Furniture
$ Good product

363.01 Mash
◊ Food & Beverage
$ Lucia's Fine Foods

363.02 Federico Landini
◊ Music
$ Nine Club

363.03 Alltagspaparazzi
• Daniel Lanzrath
◊ Design, Mobile, Photo Exhibition
$ Personal

364.01 Simon Seidel
$ Cruiseadors

364.02 Derek A. Friday
◊ Corporate & Business
$ Reed Schielke

364.03 Bleed
◊ Fashion & Lifestyle
$ By Company

364.04 &Larry
◊ Fashion & Lifestyle
$ Plush

365.01 Kokoro & Moi
◊ Public
$ Torikorttelit
$ Technology
$ AddSearch

365.02 Théo Gennitsakis
◊ Art
$ Pressure agency paris

365.03 Büro Destruct

366.01 Tyler Quarles
◊ Hospitality
$ Major Chef Restaurant Consulting

366.02 Acre
◊ Fashion & Lifestyle
$ Spur

366.03 Mikey Burton
◊ Design
$ It's The Glue

366.04 MoreSleep GmbH & Co. KG
◊ Corporate & Business
$ Freunde von Freunden

367.01 Edhv
◊ Food & Beverage
$ Treeswijkhoeve

367.02 Base
◊ Food
$ Dandoy

367.03 Mutabor Design GmbH
◊ Design
$ Mutabor Design

367.04 Csaba Bernáth
◊ Music
$ Andro

368.01 Roxane Lagache
◊ Food, Beverage, Restaurant & Private Bar
$ Hughes Piketty

368.02 Mutabor Design GmbH
◊ Corporate & Business
$ Deutsche Stimmklinik Hamburg

368.03 Noeeko – Design Studio
◊ Fashion
$ Lukas Strociak Retouching

369.01 Gytz Studio
• Henrik Gytz
◊ Cultural Institution
$ Fondet Lys

369.02 Fons Hickmann m23
◊ Cultural
$ Impulse Theater Biennale

369.03 Berger & Föhr
◊ Media, Games, & Technology
$ Modular Robotics

370.01 Ludlow Kingsley
◊ Food & Beverage
$ Grand Central Market

370.02 Ryan Feerer
◊ Furniture Design
$ Daniel Wason

370.03 Oat Creative Design Studio
• Jennifer Lucey-Brzoza
◊ Retail, Soap Company
$ Bath House

370.04 Carsten Giese | Studio Regular
• Carsten Giese, Jens Ludewig
◊ Fashion & Food Store
$ Oukan Store Berlin

371.01 Is Creative Studio
◊ Food & Beverage
$ Caravana Restaurants

371.02 Paper and Tea
• Jens De Gruyter & Evan Deterling
◊ Food & Beverage
$ P & T

371.03 Albert Naasner
◊ Fashion
$ Masomaso

371.04 Cutts Creative
• Hannah Cutts
◊ Cultural
$ Fingal head public school

372.01 Bedow Creative
◊ Music
$ More Than Human

373.01 Pierre de Belgique
◊ American Homemade Bakery
$ Captain Cook

373.02 Peter Steffen
◊ Fashion & Lifestyle
$ Fatum surfboard, Fenchurch, Cell, Fallen Hero

374.01 Pony Design Club
◊ Fashion & Lifestyle
$ Lavvus

374.02 Jonathan Sandridge
◊ Food & Beverage
$ Fields Good Chicken

374.03 Filmgraphik
◊ Music
$ Von Eden

374.04 Evelin Kasikov
◊ Design
$ Ci Evelin Kasikov

375.01 Olsson Barbieri
◊ Film & Animation
$ Animasjonsdepartementet

375.02 Bleed
◊ Music & Artist
$ Martine Kraft

375.03 Albert Naasner
◊ Fashion & Sport
$ Herbert Fleiss Sportfachgeschäft

376.01 Ian Lynam Design
◊ Cultural Institution
$ Repository for the Advanced Study of Graphic Design

377.01 Christianconlh
◊ Design
$ Personal

377.02 Rob Angermuller
◊ Corporate & Business
$ Mehnaz Alam

377.03 Longton
◊ Music & Art
$ Youth Gone

377.04 Milosz Klimek
◊ Music & Art
$ Youth Gone

378.01 21bis
◊ Corporate & Business
$ Dutchlook
378.02 Ludlow Kingsley
◊ Art, Gallery
$ Aran Cravey Gallery
378.03 Grzegorz Sołowiński
◊ Corporate & Business
$ Geszeft
378.04 Mutabor Design GmbH
◊ Coporate & Business
$ Heymann Booksellers

379.01 HappyMess Studio
• Mothi Limbu
◊ Art
$ Edition Périphérique
379.02 Commune
◊ Food & Beverage
$ Collabo-act

• Designer name, if not identical with studio name   ◊ Category $ Client   © Credits

Imprint

This book was conceived, edited, and designed by Gestalten.

Edited by Robert Klanten, George Popov, Anna Sinofzik, and Nina Müller
Interviews and foreword by Nina Müller

Cover by BMD Design for Gestalten
Layout by George Popov
Layout assistance by Michelle Kliem
Typefaces: Client Mono by Olof Linqvist, foundry: www.gestaltenfonts.com;
Dada Grotesk by deValence, foundry: www.optimo.ch

Proofreading by Felix Lennert
Printed by Printer Trento s.r.l., Trento, Italy
Made in Europe

Published by Gestalten, Berlin 2014
ISBN 978-3-89955-546-2

2nd printing, 2016

© Die Gestalten Verlag GmbH & Co. KG, Berlin 2014
All rights reserved. No part of this publication may be reproduced or transmitted in any form or by any means, electronic or mechanical, including photocopy or any storage and retrieval system, without permission in writing from the publisher.

Respect copyrights, encourage creativity!

For more information, please visit www.gestalten.com.

Bibliographic information published by the Deutsche Nationalbibliothek.
The Deutsche Nationalbibliothek lists this publication in the Deutsche Nationalbibliografie; detailed bibliographic data are available online at http://dnb.d-nb.de.

None of the content in this book was published in exchange for payment by commercial parties or designers; Gestalten selected all included work based solely on its artistic merit.

This book was printed on paper certified according to the standard of FSC®.

Gestalten is a climate-neutral company. We collaborate with the non-profit carbon offset provider myclimate (www.myclimate.org) to neutralize the company's carbon footprint produced through our worldwide business activities by investing in projects that reduce CO_2 emissions (www.gestalten.com/myclimate).